# Creative Canvaswork

Marshall Cavendish

# INTRODUCTION

At last . . . following in the footsteps of macramé, knitting, crochet and every kind of needlecraft, embroidery is enjoying an exciting new revival! Not only as the traditional craft we all know, but also as a top fashion extra, for blue jeans and shirts, jackets, bags and cushions.

Embroidery on canvas is not new. The Bayeux Tapestry is traditional canvaswork. But now the art can be used to make, not just decorate, useful, tough and hard-wearing, as well as beautiful, fashion extras for your wardrobe and for your home. *Creative Canvaswork* introduces you to embroidery on canvas, with all the basic information you will need. We tell you how to choose the right canvas for your design, how to prepare it, work it and finish it off; all the techniques for tracing patterns, working in a frame and using the varied textures of the stitches for maximum coverage and interest.

All the patterns and designs are illustrated in full colour with careful instructions, colour guides, charts and material requirements. The basic stitch library will teach you all the stitches if you are new to canvaswork and refresh your memory if you are already an expert. The many patterns for cushions, lighter and spectacle cases, hand-made personalized gifts, stool tops, picture frames, pictures, belts, bags and buckles provide the ideal practice ground for using all the traditional skills, whilst taking full advantage of all the lovely yarns, colours and textures available today.

# CONTENTS

**Photographers:**
Malcolm Aird 12, 27. Camera Press 44, 50. John Carter 52. Roger Charity 30, 31, 48. Alan Duns 27. Fabbri 1, 2, 5. Barbara Firth 8, 13, 18/19. I. Hollowood 28/29. Chris Lewis 26, 35, 42. Roger Phillips 46, 47. Renee Robinson 4. Joy Simpson 24. Peter Watkins 2.

**Designers:**
J. & P. Coats Ltd. 30, 31, 52. DMC 56. Sue Gamson 42, 46, 47. Leila Kerr 35. Susan Money 38, 39. By permission of Louis J. Gartner Jnr. & William Morrow & Co. Inc., From *Needlepoint Designs* 16, 17. Mary Rhodes & Eileen Lowcock 25, 26. Mrs. J. M. Stuart 27.

Published by Marshall Cavendish Books Limited
58 Old Compton Street London W1V 5PA

© Marshall Cavendish Limited 1970, 1971, 1972, 1973, 1974, 1975, 1976, 1977, 1978, 1979, 1980, 1981, 1982, 1983, 1984, 1985

Printed and bound by Grafiche Editoriali Padane S.p.A., Cremona, Italy

ISBN 0 86307 316 6

# Canvaswork know-how

From the time that someone called the famous Bayeux panel a tapestry, people have been confused about what is embroidery, what is tapestry and what is canvas work. In fact, the Bayeux panel is an example of early English embroidery, worked in wools on a linen fabric. Tapestry is always woven, in patterns and pictures, on a loom, with small sections woven individually, then stitched together by hand. When next you visit a museum, look carefully at the tapestries and you'll see how small some sections are. Canvas work is embroidery on canvas. It was very popular in England and Europe from the early sixteenth century until the mid-eighteenth century, but then it marked time, until it was recently revived.

Now the lovely variety of traditional canvas work stitches, which have for so long been neglected, are enjoying a new importance. They are being used in fabulous modern designs, often with unusual new yarns which were not formerly associated with embroidery.

Today, canvas work is an adventure in the use of stitches, yarns, and abstract designs which lend themselves to the square formation of the stitches.

## Colourful, textured and tough

The attraction of canvas work today, apart from the fact that it is hand-made and not mass produced, is that all-over embroidery on canvas makes objects and decorations which are really tough and hard-wearing.

It is simple to do, and you have only to visit the yarn counter of any shop to be inspired. Brilliant silks, metallic threads, stranded shiny cottons, soft matt cottons, new knobbly-textured wools and bright plastic raffia all come in a myriad of beautiful colours.

As well as the colour, the success of all canvas embroidery depends upon the texture of the stitches and the threads.

## Canvas size

The canvas must be firm, supple, and evenly woven, and the number of threads to an inch can vary from 26 per 2·5cm (1in) for fine work, to 3 per 2·5cm (1in) for very coarse work. There are two types, single thread canvas and double thread canvas. You can also use evenly woven fabrics such as Aida cloth, or Hardanger, and even-weave linens or woollen fabrics.

Single thread canvas is measured by the number of threads to 2·5cm (1in) and double thread canvas is measured to the number of double threads to 2·5cm (1in). Single weave canvas is the best to use since it is possible to embroider a wide variety of stitches on it, whereas double weave is restricted to 4 or 5 only.

## Needles

Use tapestry needles with large eyes and blunt points. They are available in a variety of sizes, of which sizes 18-21 are the most popular, but size 14 is better for very coarse material.

*Floral design, typical of nineteenth century canvas work, with soft muted colours, careful shading, and an ornate over-all appearance. Threads of canvas have been separated to produce petit point for five delicate shades.*

## Frames

Canvas work should be worked in a slate frame. This helps you to maintain the correct shape of the work while it is being embroidered. Small items which you can easily hold in your hand need not be framed.

## Yarns

In canvas work the stitches must completely cover the canvas. Threads are available in differing thicknesses and some are made up of several individual strands which are twisted together but can be separated as required. To cover the canvas you need to use the correct thickness of thread. If, however, the thread coverage looks thin and mean, you should pad it out with the technique known as tramming to fill the space. Never use too long a yarn as it will wear thin and your work will look uneven and tired. If you find the yarn becoming thin or fluffy, start a new length of yarn at once. It is usually quicker to use a short length—which is a yarn about 31cm (12in) to 36cm (14in) long.

*A modern cushion, designed by Joan Nicholson for Penelope's Simpler Range, with abstract pattern repeats, and clear bright colours*

## The right yarn for the canvas

**1. Double thread canvas**
12 double threads to 2·5cm (1in).
**Yarns:** tapestry wool, crewel wool, 4-ply knitting yarns, Pearl cotton, stranded cotton, linen embroidery thread, metallic yarns, stranded pure silk.

**2. Double thread canvas**
10 double threads to 2·5 cm (1 in).
**Yarns** as for No 1 plus double knitting yarns, plastic raffia.

**3. Coin net**
20 threads to 2·5cm (1in).
**Yarns** as for No 1.

**4. Single weave canvas**
18 threads to 2·5cm (1in).
**Yarns** as for No 1 and No 2 plus knitting yarns in a variety of textures such as mohair, tweed, metallic and wool mixtures, soft embroidery cotton, carpet thrums, Rya rug wool, applied braids and cords, spinning yarns.

**5. Single weave**
12 threads to 2·5cm (1in).
**Yarns** as for No 1 and No 2 and No 4 using more than one thickness of yarn where necessary plus fine ribbons, strings.

*Check off your canvas information against the picture on the right*

## The right stitch for the right texture

Any design loses impact if all the areas are worked in the same texture, that is, all rough or all smooth. For the most pleasing effect, it is important to separate areas of the design into smooth, medium and rough textures. (Tent, Gobelin, straight and satin stitches are all smooth. Cross stitch, rice and star stitches are all semi-rough. Double cross oblong and tufted stitches are very rough.) Some stitches lend themselves to particular textures and shapes. For instance, diagonal bricking and Smyrna cross stitch have a good texture for walls and brickwork, herringbone fillings interpret water very well and Surry stitch is a good stitch for the curves of flowers or for furry textures. Tent and Gobelin stitches clarify the line of a design and for any form of intricate, realistic shading, nothing beats tent stitch.

Strong texture often looks most effective when it is used sparingly. For example, you could work just the mane and tail of a horse in a rough textured stitch, or use different stitches for flower centres and leaves, or the underside of a fish.

## How to start

1. Find the centre of the piece of canvas by folding it in half twice; mark the centre lightly with a coloured crayon or thread. Start in the centre, but instead of using a knot, draw the needle up through the canvas, leaving a tail about 1·3cm (½in) long at the back.
2. Hold this thread closely to the canvas and work over it, binding it in with the first few stitches (which are seen here from the back).

## To finish off

Darn the thread into the stitches at the back of your work to secure it. To continue with a new thread, darn its tail into the back of the previous row.

Never allow any of these threads to accumulate in one place as this results in unsightly bumps.

## Instructions for making up canvas work

Sometimes canvas work, which takes quite a time to complete, can be ruined by hurried making up, so in order to avoid spoiling your careful work follow these instructions.

## Stretching

It is essential to allow for stretching purposes at least 5·1cm (2in) of canvas all around the finished size of the work. The excess canvas is trimmed away to the required seam width after stretching. Canvas work should never be pressed with an iron, as this flattens the textured stitches and ruins the appearance. Most stitches distort the canvas because of their diagonal pull and the best way to restore the canvas to its original shape is as follows. Dampen the back of the work with cold water. Cover a drawing board, or old work table with several sheets of white blotting paper. Place the work face down on the board and pin out, using drawing pins at 2·5cm (1in) intervals. Pull the work gently into shape, adjusting the drawing pins. Dampen the work again thoroughly and leave for at least 24 hours, away from heat, until it is dry. When the work is completely dry, check for any missed stitches and fill them in at this stage.

*This sampler is worked in tent stitch, slanted gobelin, bricking, Parisian, Hungarian, upright gobelin and slanted bricking.*

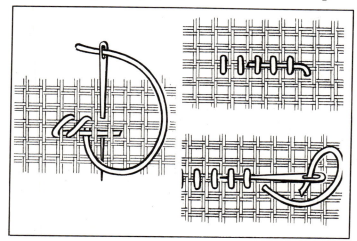

## How to make a seam

There are several seam methods suitable for canvas work and this one is particularly good for small items which cannot be turned through to the right side after being seamed. The usual seam allowance is 1·5cm (⅝in), but for smaller items, such as lighter cases, 1cm (⅜in) is sufficient. As canvas work frays easily it is a good idea to oversew the raw edges before making up. With imaginative use of yarn and stitches, the seams can form a complementary and decorative feature to the piece of work.

## Method

Trim the canvas work ready to seam and fold all turnings to the wrong side of the work. Trim and neaten the corners and tack the seam allowance in place. Pin the two seam edges with the wrong sides together, matching up the pattern. Work whip stitch, cross stitch or oblong cross stitch along the seam on the right side, picking up opposite threads of the canvas from each side as you work. The seam when completed becomes part of the canvas work.

## Linings

The choice of a lining is most important since it should not draw attention away from the stitching, either in colour or texture. It is best to choose a firm dull surface fabric in a plain toning colour. Pick the darkest tone used in the design because this will give strength to the design, whereas a light colour will draw more attention to the lining than to the canvas work. Lining seams can either be machined or hand sewn with back stitch.

## Using a chart

A chart demands a little concentration when it comes to plotting the outlines, but once these are worked out the rest is easy. Start by finding the centre of the chart. Count the number of squares from top to bottom and side to side, divide each total by half and mark the centre with a pencil or lines of tacking. Start counting and stitching from the centre. Each square on the chart corresponds to one thread intersection on the canvas. If there are large areas of colour to be filled in, mark an outline and the smaller areas first, and then fill in the larger areas.

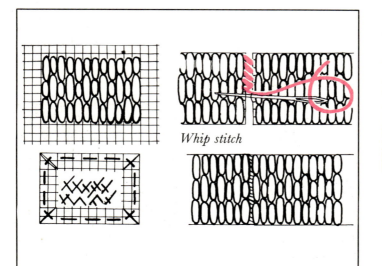

*Whip stitch*

# *Basic stitch library*

## Cross stitches

Cross stitch comes in so many guises that part of the fun of working it is to find how many adaptations you can invent. When working a sampler include as many different stitches as you can so that your work is interesting to look at. Alternatively, use one variation of cross stitch to bring a plain tent stitch picture to life.

The illustrations on these pages have been enlarged beyond life size so that each stitch is clear. When they are seen in scale the stitches will cover the canvas completely.

## Cross stitch

To work cross stitch make a row of slanting stitches from left to right and then make another row from right to left on top of them. The picture shows the stitch worked with a thin wool so that you can clearly see how it builds up but of course, worked correctly, the canvas should be completely covered with yarn. Each cross stitch should add up to a perfect square and must always be worked over an equal number of threads, down and across. The main point to remember is that the upper stitches must always lie in the same direction.

*Method of working cross stitch*

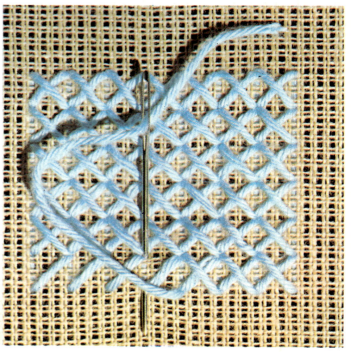

## Half cross stitch

Half cross stitch is hard-wearing—smooth, flat and ideal for things which need to be tough, like stool and chair seats. But because it is simple to do, it is one of the best stitches to use for any small scale patterns. This stitch is worked as shown, from left to right. Up through the canvas from bottom left, down through the next hole on top right. This makes a diagonal stitch on the front and a short straight stitch on the back.

Fasten off at the end of each panel of colour and begin again so that you do not leave long lengths of thread at the back.

*Half cross stitch. The drawing shows the method used when working in a frame. The right hand is always on the top of the work; the left hand at the bottom*

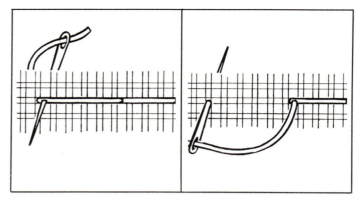

*The stitch worked over tramming*

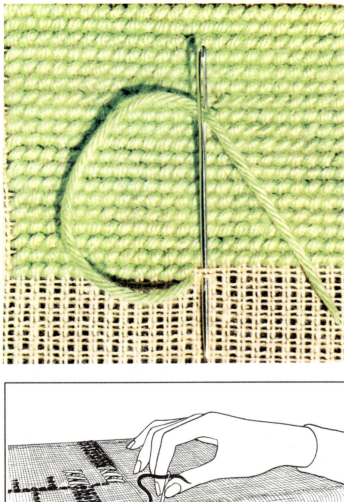

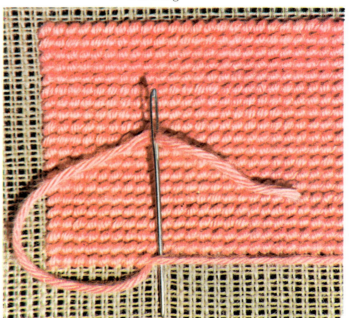

## Tent stitch or petit point

Bring the needle through to the right side and then take it back and down one thread further on. Continue to the end of the row and then work backwards and forwards until the area is filled. If the work is spread over a large area it is advisable to work the stitch diagonally to prevent the canvas being pulled out of shape. Take the needle back over 1 thread and forward 2 threads, making a longer thread on the back of the work than on the front. The stitch can also be worked in vertical or horizontal lines in alternate directions, that is, with the stitches sloping from left to right in 1 row and right to left in the next. When this method is used, it is called reversed tent stitch.

*Tent stitch—horizontal, diagonal and reversed*

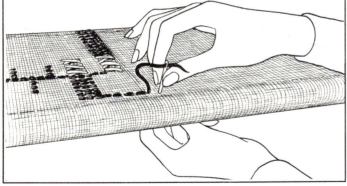

## Tramming

Tramming is a padding stitch which is used when the thread is not thick enough to cover the canvas completely.

The tramming wool runs along each horizontal single canvas thread or pairs of threads (called 'tramlines') as shown in the illustration. Bring the thread up through these tramlines, leaving the short tail at the back. Work in overlapping tramming stitches, not more than 12·7cm (4in) long for the length of your working area. Then take the thread down again through the tramlines. Work the stitch over the tramming thread, binding in the tramming tails as you go.

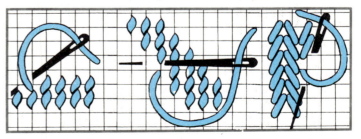

**NB** Petit-point is a smaller version of Tent stitch. The patterns in the following pages describe these as two separate stitches to make it easier to follow the charts.

## Oblong cross stitch

Work in the same way as ordinary cross stitch but bring the needle through the 5th hole down from the top of the work. Insert the needle 4 holes up, 2 across. Bring the needle through 4 holes down.

*Oblong cross stitch covers the canvas quickly and has an elegant look*

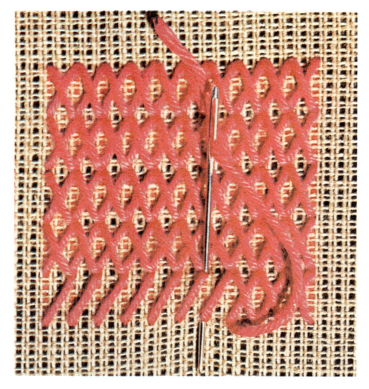

## Oblong cross stitch with bars

Begin by working oblong cross stitch then work bars one row from right to left, the next row from left to right and so on. Bring the needle through the 3rd hole down, 3rd in from the edge of work. Insert needle 2 holes back. Bring needle through 4 holes on. Repeat as above to end of row.

*Oblong cross stitch with bars for a chunkier look*

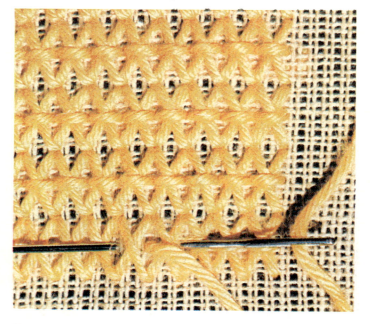

## Long legged cross stitch

This differs from ordinary cross stitch only in that one of the crossing stitches is worked over twice as many threads as the other. Bring the needle through the 4th hole down from the top of the work. Insert needle 8 holes across, 4 holes up. Bring the needle through 4 holes down. Insert needle 4 holes up, 4 back. Bring needle through 4 holes down. Repeat to the end of the row.

*Long-legged cross stitch, a simple but effective variation*

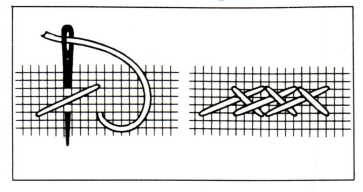

## Double cross stitch

In this stitch each star is completed before starting the next. To work one star bring the needle through at top left hand side of work. Insert needle 4 holes down, 4 across. Bring needle through 4 holes up. Insert needle 4 holes down, 4 back. Bring needle through 4 holes up, 2 across. Insert needle 4 holes down. Bring needle through 2 holes up, 2 back. Insert needle 4 holes across.

*Double cross stitch turns each stitch into an eight-pointed star*

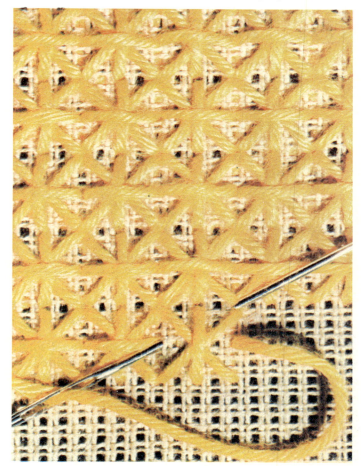

## Alternating cross stitch

This filling stitch is composed of two cross stitches of different sizes in interlocking rows.

Work from right to left. Bring needle through 3rd hole down from top of work. Insert needle 1 hole up, 1 across. Bring needle through 2 holes down. Insert needle 3 holes up, 1 across. Bring needle through 2 holes down. Repeat to end of row. To complete the crosses work the return row from left to right. Next row—bring needle through 4 holes down and work each row so that it interlocks with the one above by working the top of each stitch into the same holes as the bottom of the stitch above.

*Alternating cross stitch, a filling with lots of texture interest*

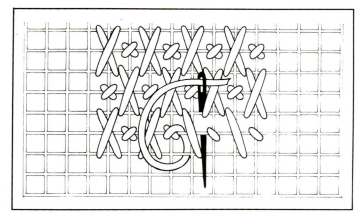

## Rice stitch

This is a filling stitch which can be worked in 1 or 2 colours (here it is shown worked in 2). It consists of ordinary cross stitch with the arms crossed by bars of half cross stitch in the same or a different colour.

Work the area in ordinary cross stitch then work the first row of bars from left to right. Bring needle through 3rd hole down from top of work. Insert needle 2 holes down, 2 across, to the right. Bring needle through 2 holes up, 2 across. Insert needle 2 holes down 2 across to the right. Repeat to the end of the row. Then repeat the process entirely from right to left to complete the row.

*Rice stitches can be worked in one colour only or two contrasting shades*

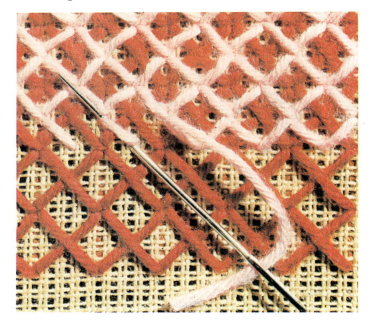

## Italian cross stitch

Work in rows from left to right, starting at the bottom left of the shape which is to be filled.

Work each stitch in 4 movements as shown in the diagram—bring needle through in the bottom left hand corner of the work. Insert needle 3 holes across. Bring needle through 1st hole again. Insert needle 3 holes up, 3 across and bring it through the 1st hole again. Insert needle 3 holes up. Bring needle through 3 holes down, 3 across. Insert needle 3 holes up, 3 back. Bring needle up 3 holes down, 3 across. Continue these movements to the end of the row, making a final upright stitch. Work another row above also from left to right. This will complete the previous row.

*Italian cross stitch sets each cross in its own square frame*

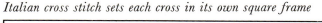
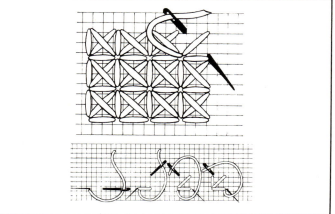

## Chain stitch

This is a very quick method worked with a fine crochet hook, missing 2 holes of the canvas with every stitch. For a shorter stitch miss 1 hole each time for a longer one miss more. Do not make the stitches too long or the work will wear badly. When one row is completed, finish off and start again with the next unless continuing in the same colour, in which case turn the work and commence the next row. It is essential to finish ends securely because if they work loose a whole row of stitching will come undone.

Work chain stitch 2 like chain stitch as shown in the illustration. Finish the end of each row with a small stitch to hold the last chain in place. Once again, finish off the thread securely.

*Chain stitch method 1*    *Chain stitch method 2*

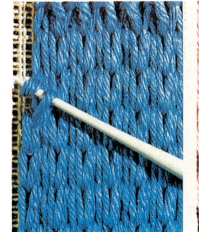

## Plaited Gobelin

This stitch is worked in horizontal rows over 4 threads up and 2 across to the left. Work to the length of the area you want to cover leaving a space of 2 threads between each stitch. The 2nd row is worked 2 threads down and is in the opposite direction, giving a plaited or woven effect.

*Plaited Gobelin Stitch*

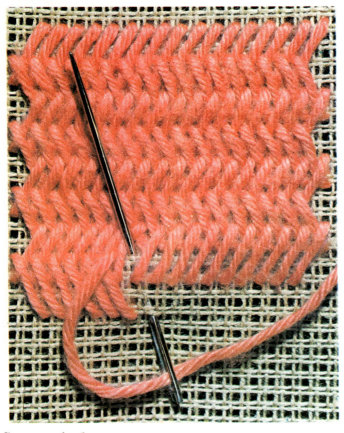

## Stem stitch

Work from the bottom upwards over 2 horizontal threads and 2 vertical threads. The spaces between the rows are filled with back stitches in a yarn of contrasting colours.

*Stem stitch*

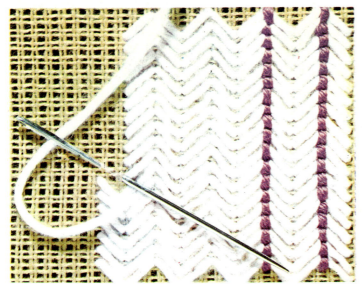

## Mosaic stitch

This is worked in diagonal rows from top left to bottom right of the canvas in groups of 3 stitches; over 1, 2, and 1 threads of canvas.

*Mosaic stitch*

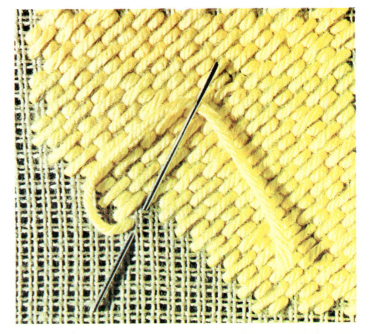

## Mosaic diamond stitch

This is worked in rows from left to right over 1, 3, 5, 3, and 1 thread of canvas.

*Mosaic diamond stitch*

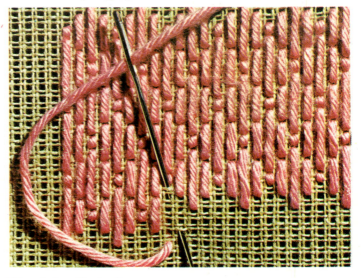

## Upright Gobelin

This is worked with straight up and down stitches, usually over 4 horizontal threads of canvas.

## Slanted Gobelin

This is similar to upright Gobelin, but worked over 2 vertical and 4 horizontal threads.

## Bricking

This upright stitch is worked in interlocking rows.

8

1 Upright gobelin
2 Slanted gobelin
3 Bricking

4 Slanted bricking
5 Parisian stitch
6 Hungarian stitch

1st row. Work alternate stitches over 4 horizontal threads leaving a space between each stitch.
2nd row. Start 2 threads lower and work a row of stitches over 4 threads, between the stitches of the first row.

## Slanted bricking
This stitch is also worked in interlocking rows, but over 2 vertical and 4 horizontal threads which gives a smooth, slanted texture.

## Parisian stitch
This is a small, close, filling stitch worked in interlocking rows, over 1 and then over 3 horizontal threads.

## Hungarian stitch
Again, this stitch is worked in interlocking rows, over 2 and then 4 horizontal threads.

## Knot stitch
This slanting stitch is worked over 3 threads of canvas and caught down with a small slanting stitch across the centre of the stitch. The rows are interlocking.

*Knot stitch: working the second stage*

## Roumanian or Roman stitch
This stitch consists of 2 rows linked with a row of stitches worked in a similar way to stem stitch. Work from left to right, and work each stitch from the top down over 6 threads and then work the central crossbar over the stitch working from right to left, 1 hole out to either side of the long stitch. Complete the row in this manner.

## Roumanian or Roman stitch 2
The second row is worked in the same way. To complete the stitch, a dividing row of stem stitch is worked from right to left, moving 1 hole to the left and 2 back all the way. This dividing row can be worked in the same colour as the main stitch, or in a contrasting colour

or yarn. On double weave canvas it creates an extremely pretty effect to work the main stitch over narrow strips of ribbon.

*Roumanian or Roman stitch, stage 1*

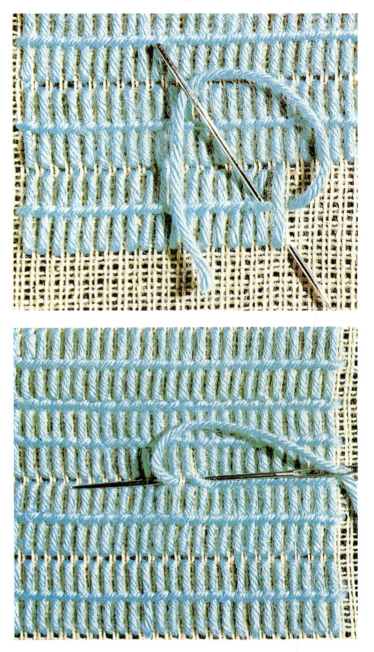

*Roumanian or Roman stitch, stage 2*

## Roman bricking
This is an interesting variation of Roumanian or Roman stitch which gives a rich braiding effect.
Work in the same manner as Roumanian stitch but going from right to left and taking the crossbar from left to right.
The second row is worked in the same way, from right to left, but interlocking the stitches by bringing out the first stitch from behind the same hole as the crossing stitch of the previous row.
This may seem a little complicated at first but the illustration should help. This stitch gives a decorative effect well worth adding to your stitch library.

*Roman bricking*

## French stitch

This very closely textured stitch is worked in diagonal rows from top left to bottom right. It makes a most attractive pattern for a background or to incorporate in a design.

Work the main stitch from the bottom up over 4 threads then a central crossbar over it from right to left. Repeat the long stitch in the same holes and then work the crossbar from left to right, starting from the same hole as the previous crossbar.

Move 4 holes down to start the next stitch.

*French stitch*

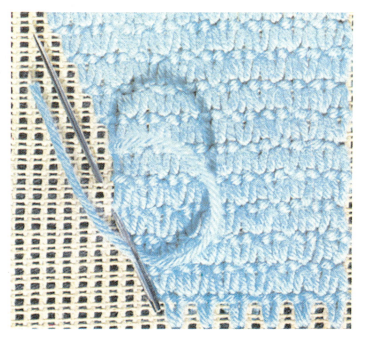

## Fern stitch

This stitch is worked downward in vertical rows.
Start from the top left of the work. Insert the needle 2 holes down and 2 across and come out again one hole to the left. Insert the needle 2 holes up and 2 across and

come out again one hole below the starting point of the previous stitch.

Continue down the length of the row and work the next one immediately alongside.

*Fern stitch*

## Rococo stitch

This stitch gives an attractive star-like pattern and makes a good background stitch. Work as for Roumanian stitch working either 3 or 4 long stitches all from the same holes but held apart by the crossbars as shown in the picture. To start the 2nd stitch bring the needle out 4 holes along from the starting point of the first stitch and fit the 2nd row in between the sections of the first row.

This stitch can be seen in the Harvest Fields sampler incorporated into the background area. You will find that this is a very useful stitch for adding texture and interest to the background of charted pictures.

*Rococo stitch*

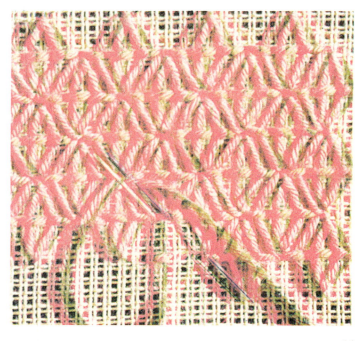

# Satin stitches

As its name suggests, satin stitch is smooth and flat. On a large piece of canvas work it is enhanced by working rough textured stitches around it, such as long-legged cross stitch. When combined with other stitches such as tent stitches or when worked to form brocade-like textures, different stitches are formed, for instance Byzantine, chequer, cushion, Florentine, Jacquard, Milanese and Moorish stitches.

It is shown in several variations in this chapter, beginning with the simple but very effective square shape of cushion stitch. See how entirely different it looks worked into a zigzag, or into a square of 4 concentric triangles for a diamond. This last version makes a lovely stylized flower head.

*Diagonal rows of satin stitch made interesting by using different colours*

### Satin stitch

The panel shows how the stitch is constructed whilst the illustration shows how it looks as a block of complete stitches.

Since satin stitch is quite long, crossing 2 or even 3 or more threads, it is not a good choice for cushions or chair covers because surfaces may catch or pull. When working with the family of satin stitches, make sure that the threads cover the canvas well, adding more strands of yarn if necessary. When using more than one strand pull them all gently to ensure an even finish.

### Cushion stitch

Before you begin working the plump squares of this stitch, decide carefully which way it is going to lie in the diagonal, its direction will make all the difference to the total effect. The diagrams show both a chequered

*How satin stitch is constructed*

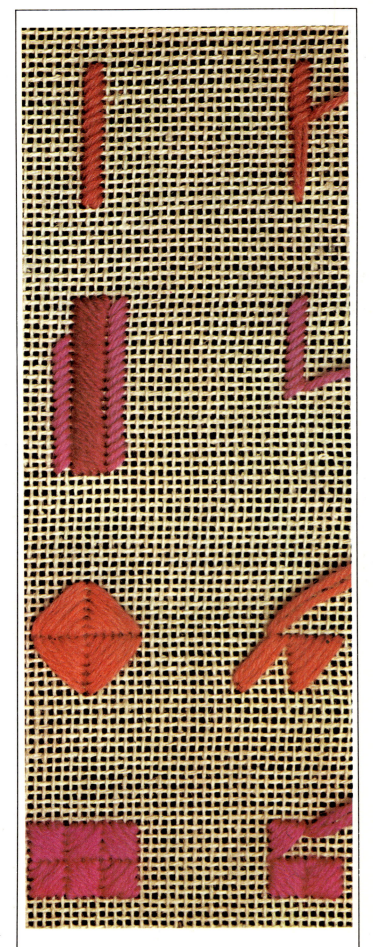

effect and a diamond effect. The diagram shows a way of padding to fill the centre gap.
Work each square in the order shown, working the diagonal stitch AB before working sections 3 and 4.

## Half cushion stitch
This is cushion stitch worked over as many threads as required until it leaves the neat triangular shape of half a square. These can be built up into diamonds.

## Diagonal satin stitch
Diagonal satin stitch worked in bands over 2 threads. This stitch can be worked in alternative directions and over a different number of threads to give interesting zigzag effects. On the right of the illustration is shown diagonal satin stitch worked over 4 and 4 threads, on the left over 2 and 4.

## Padded satin stitch
The area to be covered is first trammed and then stitched over to give a well defined padded effect.

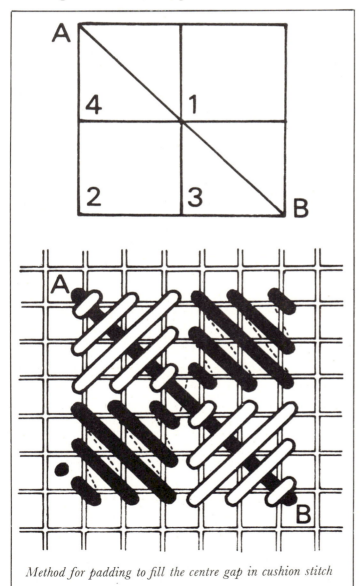

*Method for padding to fill the centre gap in cushion stitch*

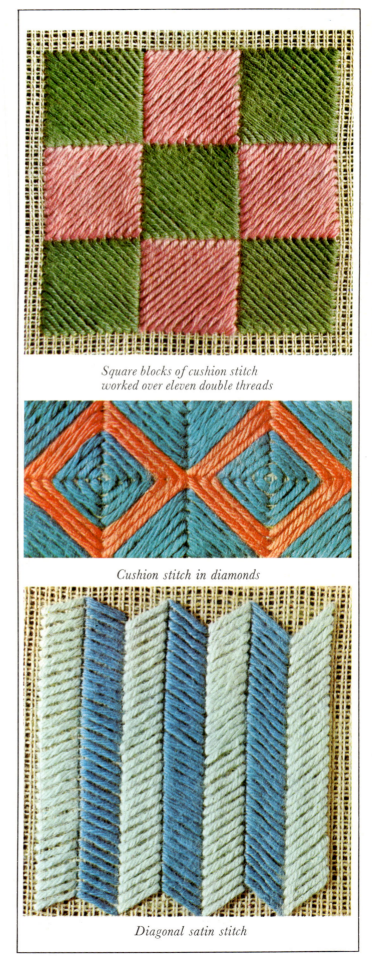

*Square blocks of cushion stitch worked over eleven double threads*

*Cushion stitch in diamonds*

*Diagonal satin stitch*

13

# Introduction to canvaswork

## Practice stitches in a sampler

The early English samplers which were made from the fifteenth to the eighteenth century are fascinating works of art, but in early Victorian days their style became rather uniform and dull. Most of them were worked entirely in cross stitch or tent stitch, using wool or silk yarns. The designs consisted mainly of the alphabet, the maker's name, her age and the date. Later they became more interesting and elaborate, frequently showing family pets and hobbies.

Modern samplers too, have progressed from the dull style of the Victorian days as shown by the exciting sampler which we illustrate, which is an adventure in colour, texture and pattern. It could be used most effectively as a wall panel but also looks marvellous as a cushion or tote bag. It is essential with canvas work to have a good practice ground for each new stitch that you learn, and it is a good idea to work two samplers at the same time, one as a practice ground and one for a clear example of each stitch.

About 2·5cm (1in) of the Harvest Fields sampler we show is missing from the right side of the picture, the complete design is shown in the diagram.

## Make a plan of action

Before beginning to make a sampler, decide on a basic plan of design and colour scheme you will use.

If this is your first attempt, you may like to copy the Harvest Fields sampler. You may on the other hand prefer to create your own design but, unless you are experienced, try to avoid difficult curves by planning a geometric design.

## Copying the design

The chart on the right shows the Harvest Fields design reduced to one third of its actual size. All you have to do is copy the chart, multiplying the measurements by 3, onto a larger sheet of graph or plain paper.

Place the copied design securely underneath the canvas, and trace in the lines using water colours and a fine brush. If this sounds too difficult, just use a ruler and a felt tip pen. It's unorthodox, but very quick and effective. This sampler is worked on single thread canvas with 18 threads to 2·5cm (1in). Make sure when you buy the canvas that it is at least 7·5cm (3in) larger than the design all around. You can use any type of canvas as long as you choose the one most appropriate to the design—coarse canvas for large shapes, and fine canvas for smaller, more intricate ones. A frame is not really necessary for working samplers of this size. Do remember that yarns give texture as well as colour, so that it is wise not to use too many colours or the effect will be muddled. Also make sure you use enough strands of yarn on the needle because the stitches must cover the canvas fully.

*Harvest Fields sampler:*

Always keep tension perfectly even so that the design is not distorted.

## Yarns and colours

The list gives the complete range of yarns for the sampler, but if you are planning your own design you can experiment with unusual yarns as much as you like. Mix silks with wool or try a fluffy textured wool with the smooth texture of raffia—or make it more exciting with a border of ribbons or beads.

## Go to town on texture

One stitch pattern for the Harvest Fields sampler is suggested in the diagram, but of course you may want to plan your own. Each stitch pattern gives a different texture, so when making a sampler, be sure to arrange the textures in a balanced composition. Mix them well, and avoid using all the smooth textures on the one side and all the rough ones on the other.

| | | greens | yellows | oranges |
|---|---|---|---|---|
| Anchor | soft embroidery | | | |
| | cotton | 0280 (1) | 0288 (2) | |
| | stranded embroidery | | | |
| | cotton | 0279 (1) | 0298 (2) | 0308 (1) |
| | tapestry wool | 0279 (6) | | |
| | | 0423 (2) | | |
| | | 0422 (4) | | |
| | | 0424 (2) | | |
| | | 0424 (2) | | |
| Penelope | crewel wool | | 571 (4) | 611 (4) |

(numbers in brackets = skeins)

You will also need one ball of tweed-texture knitting wool and a skein of cocoa-coloured plasticised raffia.

*Area up to arrow shown opposite*

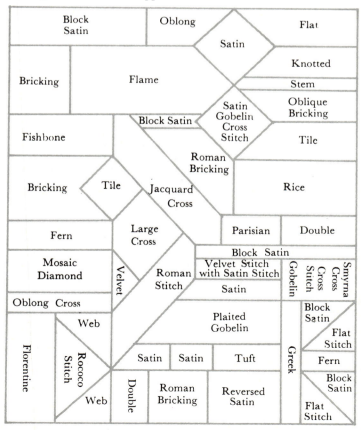

# Cats in canvaswork

Louis J. Gartner, who designed and executed these realistic looking pieces of canvas work, makes up his designs by 'borrowing' the elements, sometimes from magazine and book illustrations.

The leopard cub was taken from a magazine illustration and enlarged life size to fit into a 36·5cm (14in) diameter circle. The original picture was full of small detail which decided the designer to work the animal itself in petit point against a gros point background. To reproduce the plump roundness of a live animal and the subtlety of the baby fur, Louis J. Gartner used twelve different 'fur' coloured yarns plus black and white. The shaded background to the animal was achieved by working colours in slanting stripes, so that the tones blended imperceptibly, giving an effect of space behind the cub.

With a little practise and imagination it is possible to reproduce almost anything in this way making use of the stitches in your stitch library. The delightful thing about canvas work is that it is adaptable and easy to work, and the pieces you produce which are all your own are those which will give the greatest satisfaction, and may become the collector's pieces of tomorrow.

*This tiger's head was designed and executed by Louis J. Gartner. The design was 'borrowed' from an album sleeve design.*

# Covering a stool in canvas

If a favourite stool shows signs of wear on the top fabric, it is relatively simple to work a new top in canvas work to re-cover it. The stitches used in the design shown here suggest stripes. The stitches chosen are chain stitch method 1, chain stitch method 2 and plaited Gobelin and some stem stitch (see diagrams). Canvas work is particularly suitable for stool tops because it is so hard wearing. For the best results the important thing to bear in mind is always to use the best quality yarns and linen canvas. Also, special care must be taken when planning the design as this must view equally well from every angle.

## For the stool top
### You will need
☐ Linen canvas (to assess amount required measure across the width of the stool plus the drop on both sides. Measure in the same way for the length and add 15cm (6in) to each measurement to allow for stretching).
☐ Muslin of a similar amount
☐ Soft lead pencil
☐ Dressmaking pins
☐ Tapisserie wool or crewel wool in the amounts specified for the design chosen
☐ Tapestry needle No 18
☐ Fine 1·3cm (½in) upholstery tacks for corners
☐ Brass headed upholstery tacks (sufficient to go around the stool placed close together.

## Before you begin
Remove the old covering and make sure that the existing padding is firm and even. If not, the top should be re-upholstered.

## Making a pattern
Working out the shape of the pattern is first done with muslin, just like a toile in dressmaking. The muslin must be big enough to more than cover the seat area and the drop. Use a soft pencil, mark a vertical and a horizontal line from side to side across the centre of the muslin, using the thread of the weave as a guide. Draw similar lines in the centre of the stool. Position the muslin on the stool, matching the lines. Pin the muslin to the stool top, starting at the centre of the crossed lines and working out simultaneously to all 4 sides, placing the pins at 7·5cm (3in) intervals. Continue these lines of pins down the depth of the drop. Pin the corners to make mitres. With a soft pencil, mark the area of the top of the stool, the edge of the frame and both sides of each mitred corner. Take the muslin off the stool and measure the length and width of the muslin to make sure that it corresponds exactly to the measurements of the stool. If it does not, the muslin has been pulled out of shape. Working on a firm surface, pin the muslin onto brown paper, making sure that the weave of the muslin is straight. The pattern on the muslin may be slightly irregular but make the

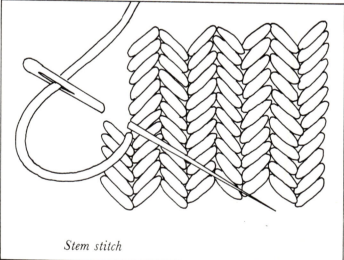

*Stem stitch*

brown paper absolutely symmetrical. Mark the vertical and horizontal lines on the canvas to match up with those on the paper pattern. Pin the pattern to the canvas and mark with a felt pen round the edge. This gives the area of the canvas to be worked. Cut the canvas to a square leaving at least a 7·5cm (3in) margin all around for stretching.

## Covering the stool
When you have completed stitching the design on the canvas for the stool cover, stretch and trim the work, leaving the unworked areas of canvas in the corners for mitring. Turn the seam allowances to the back of the

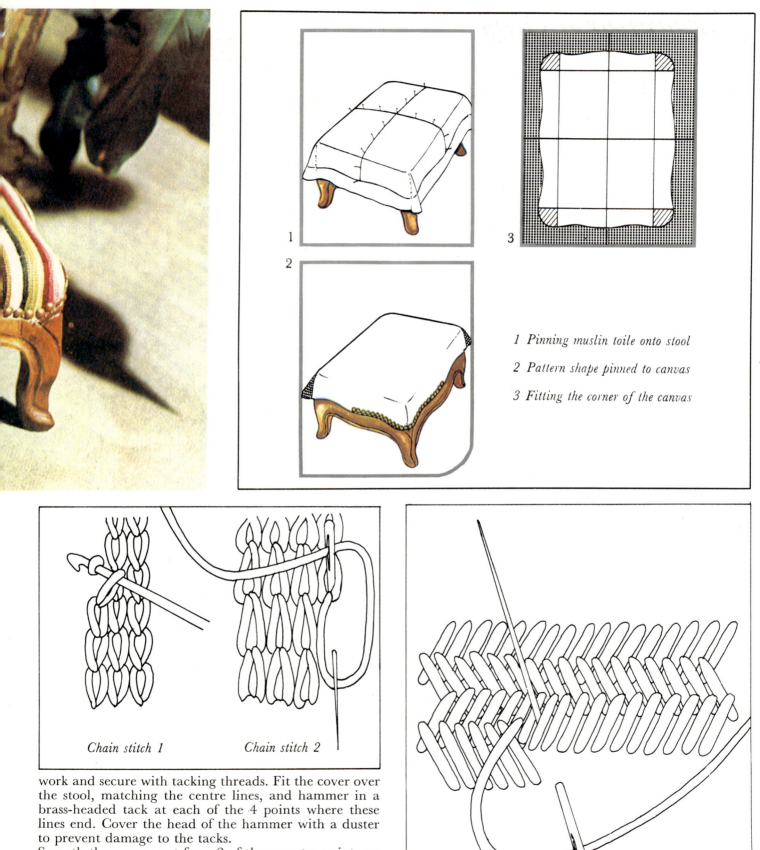

1 Pinning muslin toile onto stool

2 Pattern shape pinned to canvas

3 Fitting the corner of the canvas

*Chain stitch 1*     *Chain stitch 2*

*Plaited Gobelin stitch*

work and secure with tacking threads. Fit the cover over the stool, matching the centre lines, and hammer in a brass-headed tack at each of the 4 points where these lines end. Cover the head of the hammer with a duster to prevent damage to the tacks.

Smooth the canvas out from 2 of these centre points on adjacent sides, working towards the corner and tacking with brass-headed tacks as you go. Fix the point of the canvas corner to the stool using an upholstery tack then ease the edges of the worked canvas together to meet at the corner edge (see diagram).

Work the remaining corners in the same way, working the diagonally opposite corner next.

# Belts made with cross stitch

Despite its simplicity, cross stitch can be extremely effective and adaptable. These patterns for example, make marvellous belts and borders. It is fascinating to experiment with colour schemes because a design originally in one colour combination will look entirely different in another.

## For the belts
### You will need
To obtain a design about $\frac{2}{3}$ of the size of the motifs illustrated, use double thread canvas with 14 threads to 2·5cm (1in) and tapestry wool, stranded cotton or a soft embroidery cotton. You can adapt designs to coarser or finer canvas, using appropriately thicker or finer yarns.

## Orange and brown design
This is a simple pattern using square motifs in 3 colours. Try using 3 tones of one colour or, for a chequerboard effect, use a black background with grey and white centres. For an all over design, the square motifs could be grouped to form geometric designs and with an interesting use of colour against a contrasting background shade, a fascinating patchwork effect can be achieved.

*Orange and brown design*

## Red and gold design
This motif lends itself to being repeated over a large area and readily adapts itself for a cummerbund, bag, stool top, cushion or chair seat. Make an exotic waistcoat in gold, copper and silver metallic yarns.

*Red and gold design*

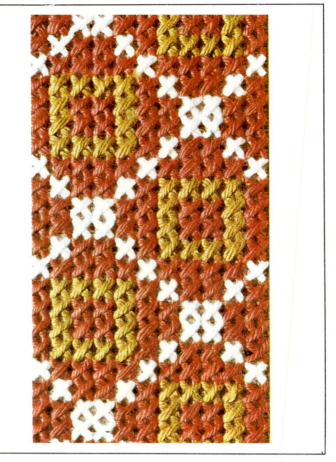

## Pink and green trefoils
Use half cross stitch or tent stitch for this pretty design. If you make this up in a different combination of colours, the whole character of the design becomes more sophisti-

*Pink and green trefoils*

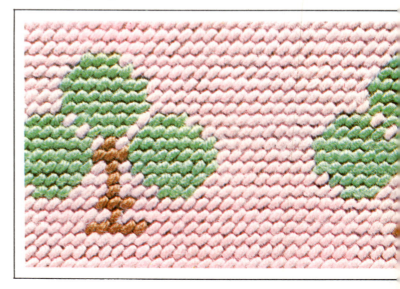

cated. To add more texture, you could work either the background or the trefoils in tiny cross stitch, or tram the trefoils to give a raised effect.

## Blue and brown design

This L-shaped repeat motif is stitched in upright Gobelin stitch worked over 4, 3 and 2 double threads of canvas. The background is worked over 1 thread. A three-dimensional effect is obtained by using tones of one colour for the L-shape. This motif can be adapted to build up geometric designs.

*Blue and brown design*

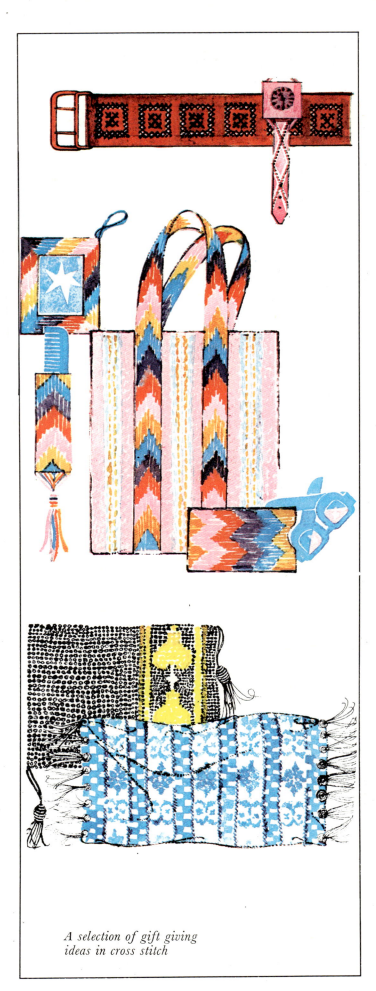

*A selection of gift giving ideas in cross stitch*

# Follow
# the band

Canvas work has recently been updated by working it in brilliant colours for fashion accessories. The belts and bands given here are worked on double thread canvas with 10 double threads to 2·5cm (1in). Tent stitch is used throughout. All colours and numbers refer to Patons Beehive Tapestry Wool.

## For the neckband
**Finished size—5cm (2in) deep by
neck measurement**

**You will need**
- [ ] Canvas 15·2cm (6in) by 56cm (22in)
- [ ] 0·45m (½yd) ribbon, 5cm (2in) wide
- [ ] 61cm (24in) leather thonging
- [ ] 2 hanks each of red No 2502, purple No 2522, lilac No 2524, black No 2622, orange No 2592, yellow No 2580. **NB** Lilac is shown on the chart as white for clarity.

## Method of working
Work the design from the chart for the required length. Stretch and trim the canvas. Turn the raw canvas on the long sides to the back of the work and catch them down with herringbone stitch. To make the channel through which the thonging slots, turn the raw canvas on the two ends to the back of the work and back stitch them down, 1cm (⅜in) from the edge. Line the band with ribbon using slip stitches and working through only one thickness of canvas at the ends so that the thonging channel is left open. Slot the thonging upwards through one channel and downwards through the other (see illustration).

## For the fringed girdle
**Finished size—8·2cm (3¼in) deep by the waist measurement, taken loosely plus 16·5cm (6½in) overlap, for a wider belt use coarser canvas**

**You will need**
- [ ] Canvas 18cm (7in) by 91cm (36in)
- [ ] Lining 10cm (4in) by 91cm (36in)
- [ ] 6 hanks each of red No 2511, lilac No 2524; 3 hanks each of purple No 2526, yellow No 2579; 2 hanks each of black No 2622, orange No 2592.
- [ ] Piece of card 8·2cm (3¼in) by 15cm (6in)
- [ ] Large press studs.

## Method of working
Work the design from the chart for the required length. Stretch and trim the canvas. Fold under the raw canvas and herringbone stitch into place. To make the fringe wind wool for 7·5cm (3in) along the card. Carefully sew one end of the loops to the canvas 0·6cm (¼in) in from the end of the girdle, making sure that every strand is included. Slide the card out and work a row of back stitches to secure the fringe. Complete work by lining

the girdle, enclosing the ends of the fringe. Use press studs for fastening, laying one end of the girdle over the other (see illustration).

## For the thonged belt
**Finished size—6·4cm (2½in) deep by the waist measurement, loosely taken**

**You will need**
- [ ] Canvas 16·5cm (6½in) by 91cm (36in)
- [ ] Lining 10cm (4in) by 91cm (36in)
- [ ] 114cm (45in) leather thonging
- [ ] 10 eyelets and eyelet tool
- [ ] 4 hanks orange No 2591; 3 hanks red No 2594; 7 hanks lilac No 2521.

## Method of working
Work the design from the chart for the required length. Stretch and trim the canvas. Fold under the raw canvas and herringbone stitch into place. Line the belt and then insert 5 eyelets vertically, evenly spaced on each end of the belt. Lace the thonging through and tie.

*A belt with leather thonging laces and a detail of thonging*

*The neckband with leather thonging tie*

## For the wristband
**Finished size—5cm (2in) deep by wrist measurement**

### You will need
- ☐ Canvas 15cm (6in) by 25cm (10in)
- ☐ 0·25m (¼yd) ribbon, 5cm (2in) wide
- ☐ 61cm (24in) leather thonging
- ☐ 1 hank each of the colours given for the neckband.

### Method of working
Work the same way and to the same design as for the neckband.

*Wristband to match the neckband and girdle*

*A fringed girdle to wear with a simple dress*

Chart for matching wristband, neckband and fringed girdle    Chart for the leather thonged belt

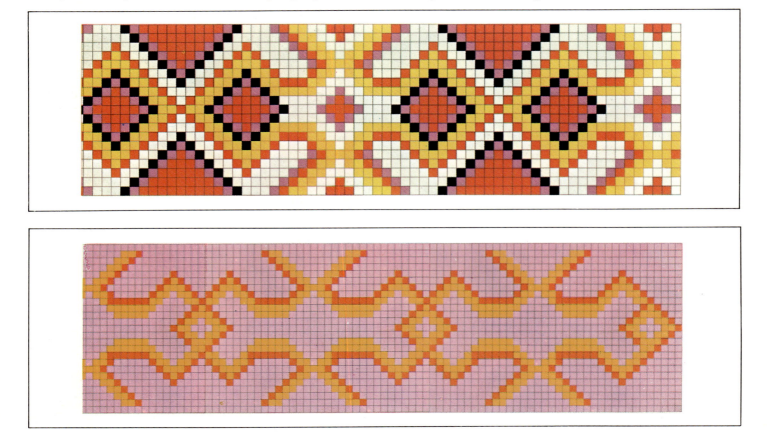

23

# Make a lighter or spectacle case

If you are not yet very experienced at canvas work you will find that both lighter and spectacle cases are quick, fun and easy to make. You can try out your favourite stitch to work an all over, rich textured pattern, or you can use any of the other stitches you have learned.

## For the spectacle case
### You will need
☐ Canvas
☐ Yarn
☐ 10cm (4in) length of cord
☐ Lining

### Method of working
Cut the canvas to measure 46·2cm (18¼in) by 17cm (6¾in), and cover an area which measures 36·9cm (14½in) by 7cm (2¾in) with stitches.
Stretch and trim the canvas, then cut a piece of lining material to the trimmed size. To prepare the canvas work for seaming, fold lengthways leaving a 6·4cm (2½in)

flap, right sides facing.
Stitch the piece of cord securely to the seam allowance on the wrong side, 2·5cm (1in) down from the opening. Tack edges and seam.
With right sides of the lining together, turn up 16·2cm (6⅜in) leaving a 7·4cm (2⅞in) flap. Stitch the side seams from the fold to within 1cm (⅜in) of the opening. Fold the seam allowance round the flap and across the opening to the wrong side of the lining, tack and press. Slip the lining into the case, using a blunt pencil to push it right down into the corners. Pin the lining round the edges of the opening and flap, matching the seams of the lining to the seams of the case, and tack them together and slip stitch neatly into place. Remove tacking. Fold over the 6·4cm (2½in) flap and tuck it under the cord.

## For the lighter case
### You will need
☐ Canvas
☐ Yarn
☐ Lining

### Method of working
For an average size lighter case, cut the canvas to measure 17cm (6¾in) by 25·4cm (10in) and embroider an area measuring 7cm (2¾in) by 15·2cm (6in). Stretch the canvas and prepare it for seaming. With the right side of the work facing you, fold it in half and stitch the side seams, finishing as described for the spectacle case, omitting the flap and cord.

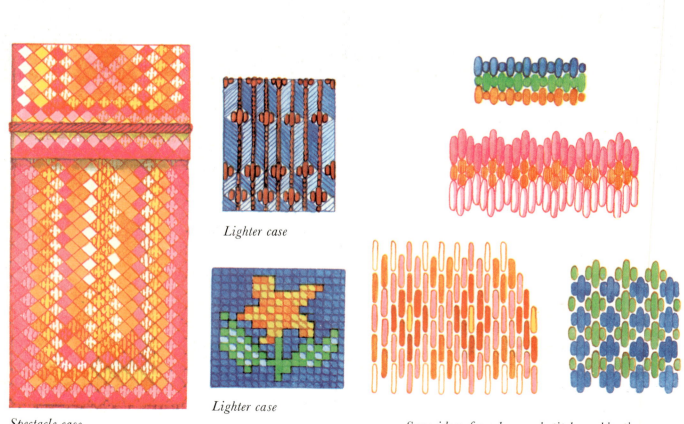

Spectacle case

Lighter case

Lighter case

Some ideas for colour and stitch combinations

# More small gifts to make

*A simple wild pansy purse worked in three stitches*

Many people who might be tempted to try their hand at canvaswork are daunted by the large pieces of work they see in shops and magazines. Although these large pieces can provide inspiration, the inexperienced embroiderer needs encouragement in the form of smaller simple pieces. These should be well designed and colourful enough to be fun to make and pleasing to give.

Any of the canvas work articles shown here should be simple enough to be worked by someone new to this form of embroidery—or might be worked just as effectively in more complex stitches by the experienced embroiderer.

A tiny wild pansy inspired the motif for the change purse in canvaswork and the spectacle case is based upon an abstract form of the same shape. The design for the purse has been kept very simple and all unnecessary detail omitted. The central motif is outlined with a felt tipped pen and traced through onto the canvas. The natural colours of the flower are worked in three stitches: tent stitch for the outline of the design, small diagonal stitch for the flower and mosaic stitch.

The flower shape has been further simplified for the spectacle case and the resulting design is more stylized. The central figures are worked in cross stitch, and cushion stitch is used for the background. When the stitchery has been completed, stretch the canvas over a thin piece of card cut to the shape required, glueing the turnings to the reverse side for the lining of the spectacle case.

The design can be repeated on the reverse side of the case, or the reverse side can be worked in cushion stitch in just one toning colour. After stitching the 2 sides of the spectacle case together, cover the join with velvet ribbon or cord. Alternatively, work an edge stitch round each piece of canvas, then stitch the 2 sides together. The tiny lighter case is a simple rectangular strip of canvas worked in a variation of bricking stitch, folded in half and sewn up along the sides. An edge stitch finishes off the piece along the folded edges.

## Making a pincushion

1. Choose a simple motif or design for a square or rectangular pincushion and make a chart on graph paper before beginning to work.

Each small square on the chart represents one stitch.

A combination of stitches will provide a pleasing contrast in texture. For instance tent, Gobelin, straight and satin stitches are all smooth. Cross stitches rice and star are all semi-rough. Double cross, oblong and tufted stitches are very rough. Remember that strong texture is often most effective when used in small areas.

2. A monogram or single letter is easy to work out on a chart, and makes a particularly appealing pincushion. The letter or letters might be worked in tent stitch and the background in cushion stitch or alternating rows of tent stitch and long-legged cross stitch. Use Anchor Tapisserie wools and work on single weave canvas with 14 threads to 2·5cm (1in), using a No 20 tapestry needle.

3. After the design has been worked, stretch the canvas and trim off the excess, allowing 1·6cm (⅝in) turnings. For the backing, cut a square or rectangle of velvet or other sturdy fabric to the size of the trimmed canvas. Tack the turnings to the wrong side to make a neat, accurate square or rectangle. Tack the canvas turnings to the back of the work and pin the velvet to the canvas, wrong sides together. Hem the velvet firmly into place, stitching into the outer row of canvaswork stitches. Leave half of one side open for stuffing. Bran, sheepswool and emery powder are all suitable materials for stuffing and should be packed very tightly. Close the opening with pins and hem tightly when fully stuffed. Neaten by sewing cord all around the edge, covering seam.

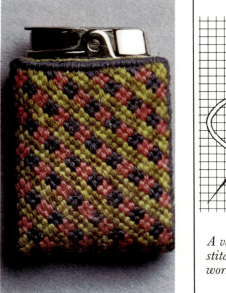

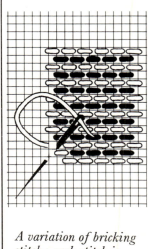

*A variation of bricking stitch; each stitch is worked over two threads*

△ *A single stitch is used for this tiny lighter case*

◁ *Rich colours and an elegant design for spectacle case*

▽ *Other gift giving ideas in canvaswork*

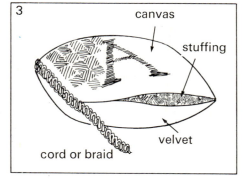

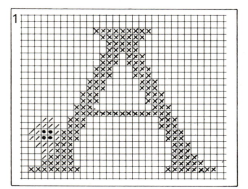

1

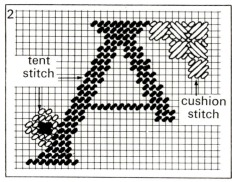

2 tent stitch

cushion stitch

3 canvas

stuffing

cord or braid

velvet

26

# A pincushion for the apple of your eye

A pin cushion is a good way to begin working from a charted picture. This is less expensive than choosing a painted or trammed canvas, which will confine you to the most commercially available designs, while a charted picture gives you the opportunity of picking your own colours and building up your own designs. For instance, you can repeat the apple motif given below at random all over a cushion or turn it into a yellow Golden Delicious or a green Granny Smith.

## Apple Pincushion

This plump apple pincushion uses lustrous cushion stitch to interpret the shiny apple, rough reinforced cross stitch

*Two pincushions to work: one from the chart below, one row by row*

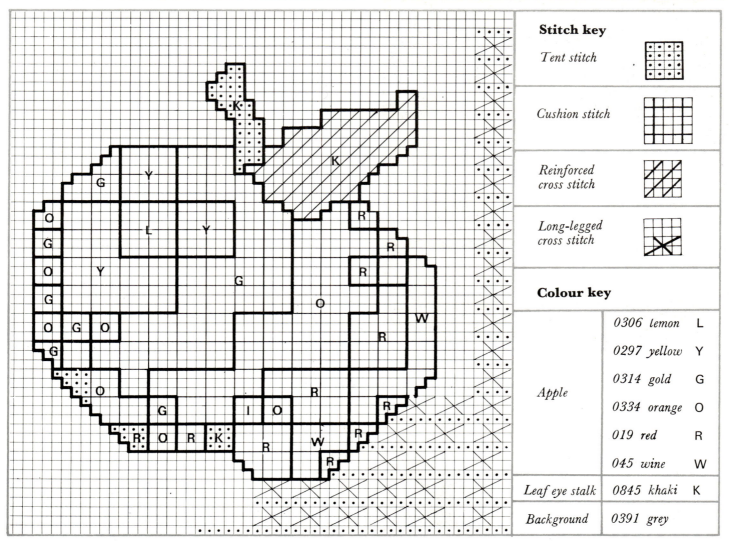

**Stitch key**

| | |
|---|---|
| *Tent stitch* | |
| *Cushion stitch* | |
| *Reinforced cross stitch* | |
| *Long-legged cross stitch* | |

**Colour key**

| | | | |
|---|---|---|---|
| | 0306 | lemon | L |
| | 0297 | yellow | Y |
| *Apple* | 0314 | gold | G |
| | 0334 | orange | O |
| | 019 | red | R |
| | 045 | wine | W |
| *Leaf eye stalk* | 0845 | khaki | K |
| *Background* | 0391 | grey | |

for the gnarled leaf, and precise tent stitch for the neat shape of the stalk and eye.

## For the apple pincushion
### You will need

☐ Single weave canvas 25·4cm (10in) by 25·4cm (10in), 14 threads ro 2·5cm (1in). (Finished size about 10·2cm (4in) square.)
☐ No 20 tapestry needle and a sharp needle for sewing up.
☐ Velvet or other backing material 15·2cm (6in) by 15·2cm (6in). One skein of Anchor Tapisserie wools 0306, 0297, 0314, 0334, 019, 045, 0845; and 2 skeins of 0391.
☐ 40·6cm (16in) of cord for trimming.
☐ For filling, bran from the corn merchants, or sawdust.

### Method of working
Prevent the canvas from fraying by cutting strips of brown paper and tacking them over the edges. On the chart each square represents 1 canvas thread crossing which is to be covered by a single tent stitch.
Apple: Work in cushion stitch in groups of 4, over 3 threads.
Eye and Stalk: Work in tent stitch over 1 thread.
Leaf: Work in reinforced cross stitch (i.e. cross stitch worked twice over) over 2 threads. This ensures that there is a good coverage of the canvas.
Background: Work in alternate rows of long-legged cross stitch worked over 2 threads, and tent stitch worked over 1 thread.
NB To clarify chart, background symbols do not cover entire area.

### Stretching the canvas back in shape
When the design is completed stretch the canvas and trim off excess canvas allowing 1·6cm ($\frac{5}{8}$in) turnings.

### Finishing off
To back the cushion, cut a square of velvet to the size of the trimmed canvas. Tack the turnings to the wrong side to make a neat accurate square. Tack canvas turnings to back of work. Pin velvet to canvas, wrong sides together and whip the velvet firmly into place.
Leave half of one side open for stuffing.
Bran is the stuffing which best allows pins to be pushed in easily. Pack it in very tightly—a teaspoon will help. Close the opening with pins and whip tightly when fully stuffed. Brush off any bran left lying on the pincushion. Neaten by sewing cord all around the edge.

## Square pincushion
### Method of working
The square pincushion is worked in delightful, bright, rich colours in a simple geometric design using a variety of lovely stitches. Work it outwards from a centre block of 4 cushion stitches in rows as follows: 2 rows tent stitch, 1 row cross stitch, 1 row Smyrna cross stitch, 1 row satin stitch, 1 row cross stitch (oblong with bars), 1 row long-legged cross stitch, 1 row Smyrna cross stitch, 1 row satin stitch, 1 row cross stitch. For the sides work 1 row oblong cross stitch with bars, 1 row long-legged cross stitch, 1 row Smyrna stitch, 1 row long-legged cross stitch, 1 row oblong cross stitch with bars. Work long-legged cross stitch for seams.

# Canvaswork cover story

Snap-on covers are just the thing to update a favourite clutch bag, either for day or evening wear. Cover the canvas with smooth satiny textures for smart occasions, rich, tweedy textures for country wear, or glittering gold or silver for evening wear. One basic bag can have a wardrobe of inter-changeable covers. Two interesting stitch combinations are given in this chapter.

## For the canvaswork cover
### You will need
☐ A plain clutch bag.
☐ Sufficient canvas to cover the bag plus 5cm (2in) extra all around for stretching and seam allowances

- Piece of lining the same size as the canvas
- 6 large press studs
- Embroidery yarn
- Tapestry needle
- Strong paper.

## Making the pattern

Measure the width of the bag and then measure the length from the front flap edge, up the front of the bag, over the top and down to the back edge. Draw a rectangle to these measurements on the paper and cut out the pattern of the outline.

Pin the pattern onto the canvas, making sure to follow the grain of the canvas. Mark the pattern outline with either tacking stitches or a felt tipped pen. Find the canvas centre by making two lines of tacking stitches, one along the centre lengthwise and the other across the centre widthways.

## Plan the design and stitches to be used

## Method of working

Work the required area of stitching on the canvas,

working out from the centre as marked by the crossed lines of tacking. When the embroidery is completed stretch the canvas. Trim the canvas to within 1·5cm (⅝in) of the stitching.

## To make up

Cut the piece of lining the same size as the trimmed canvas. Fold the raw canvas seam allowance to the back of the work and tack in place. Turn 1·5cm (⅝in) to the wrong side of lining and press. Place the canvas and the lining wrong sides together and tack all round the edge. Stitch the 2 pieces together using a small slip stitch,

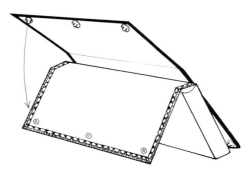

*Sew press studs on bag and cover*

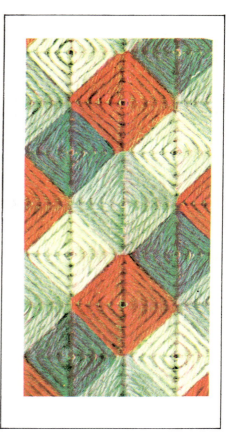

*Half cushion stitch*

*A simple clutch bag glamorized with a snap-on canvas work cover*

29

remove tacking.

Attach large press studs, positioned as shown with one half of the stud on the bag and the other half on the underside of the cover.

## Cushion stitch and cross stitch

The stitches used for the bag cover illustrated are large cushion stitch and cross stitch. The cushion stitch is made up of 15 stitches and the cross stitch worked over 2 double threads of canvas each way. To prevent too long a stitch, work on either double thread canvas, with 15 double threads to 2·5cm (1in), or single thread canvas with 18 threads to 2·5cm (1in). For a more decorative finish the edge has been covered with narrow braid.

*Cushion stitch and cross stitch combine to make an interesting pattern*

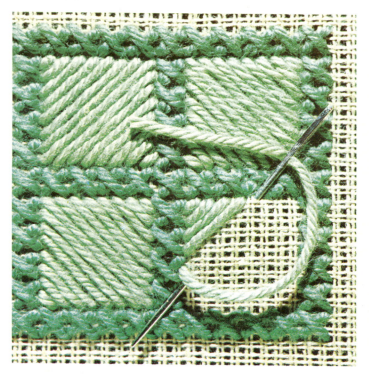

## Algerian filling

This filling is made up of small blocks of satin stitch, in this case groups of 3 stitches worked over 4 double threads of canvas. The same stitch can be worked equally well on single thread canvas. It can either be worked entirely in one colour to form a textured background or in complementary colours to form a pattern.

*Algerian filling looks interesting when worked in a variety of colours*

# Canvaswork shoulder bag

This practical shoulder bag features an original canvas-work panel in a bold geometric design, worked in subtle shades. Simple enough for a beginner to make, the canvaswork is backed with a sturdy fabric in a toning colour.

**For the bag**
**approx 25cm (10in) square with 5cm (2in) wide gusset and strap:**

## You will need

☐ 0.45m (½yd) by 58·3cm (23in) wide single thread canvas, 18 threads to 2·5cm (1in)
☐ Anchor Tapisserie Wool, 5 skeins 0280 muscat green; 4 skeins 0850 petrol blue; 3 skeins 0386 cream; 2 skeins each 0423 olive green and 0849 light petrol blue
☐ Tapestry frame
☐ Milward 'Gold seal' tapestry needle No 18
☐ 0·90m (1yd) cotton twill, denim, canvas or similar fabric
☐ 0·90m (1yd) lining fabric in a toning colour
☐ 0·90m (1yd) iron-on Vilene
☐ Sewing thread to match fabric

## Method of working

Mark the centre of the canvas horizontally and vertically with a line of tacking stitches and mount on the tapestry frame. The working chart gives the complete design with the bisecting lines indicated by arrows outside the design. These should coincide with the tacking stitches.

The design is worked in cross stitch, chain stitch and petit point. Each square on the chart represents 2 threads of canvas and the stitch details indicate the number of threads over which each stitch is worked. Begin the work centrally and follow the key to determine which stitches and colours to use. If required, the worked canvas may be dampened, then pinned and stretched to the correct shape on a clean dry board, using rustproof drawing pins. Leave the canvas to dry naturally for 2 to 3 weeks.

## To make up the bag

Trim the canvas all round to within 2·5cm (1in) of the worked area and mitre the corners. Cut a square of fabric to match the size of the worked canvas, allowing 1·3cm (½in) all round for turnings.

Cut the gusset (the base and sides) of the bag as one piece and cut a matching strip of fabric for the shoulder strap. This strip should measure 7·6cm (3in) by approximately 81cm (32in), but adjust the length of the strap to fit.

Using the four components of the bag (front, back, gusset and strap) as patterns, cut matching pieces of lining fabric and iron-on Vilene. Press the Vilene to the back of each piece of fabric, first pressing back the turnings of the shoulder strap only. Do not apply Vilene to the worked canvas yet.

With right sides together, machine stitch across both ends of the long strips of fabric. Before doing this, check the measurements once again to make certain that the 2 seams between the gusset and the shoulder strap will coincide exactly with the top edge of the worked canvas. Place the right side of the gusset against the worked surface of the canvas and machine stitch around three sides of the canvaswork design. This row of stitching should be 1 or 2 rows in from the edge to make certain that no exposed canvas appears. In order to machine through the canvas smoothly, it is advisable to place a few sheets of tissue paper between the machine plate and the back of the canvas. Press back 2·5cm (1in) of unworked canvas and place Vilene (trimmed to exact size

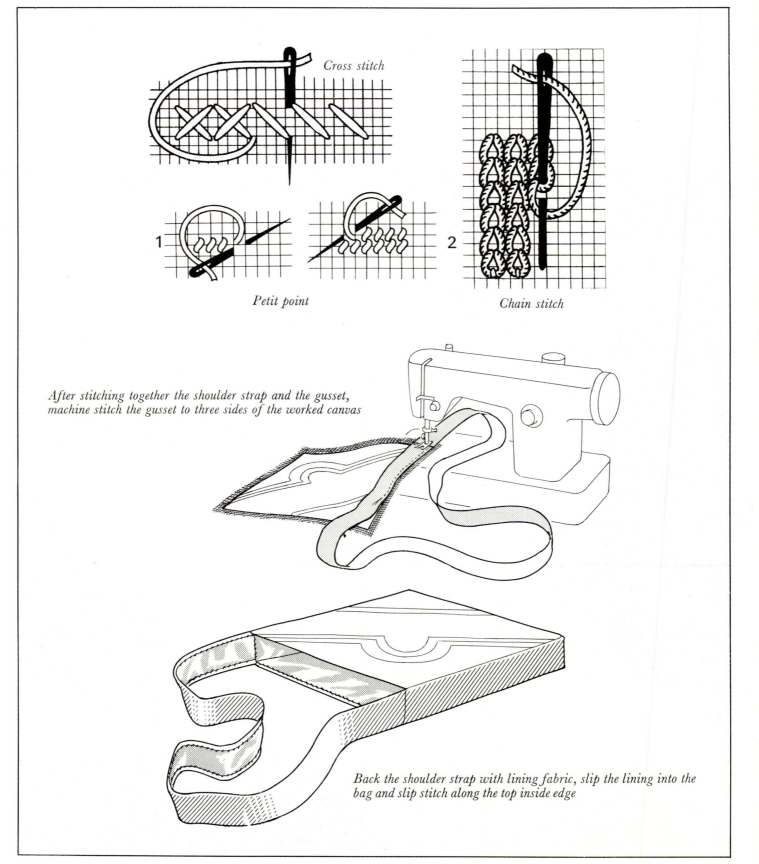

*Cross stitch*

*Petit point*

*Chain stitch*

*After stitching together the shoulder strap and the gusset, machine stitch the gusset to three sides of the worked canvas*

*Back the shoulder strap with lining fabric, slip the lining into the bag and slip stitch along the top inside edge*

of the worked area) over the back of the canvas covering the turnings. Iron on the Vilene. Press back the turnings along one side of the fabric back of the bag and machine stitch the gusset to this piece as before. Turn right side out.

Stitch together the front, back and gusset of the lining fabric with right sides together and press back the turnings. Tack the remaining strip of lining fabric to the inside of the shoulder strap and hem stitch along both sides. Slip the lining into the bag and hem stitch along the top edge.

To complete the bag, tuck the ends of the shoulder strap lining under the lining of the bag at each side and secure with hem stitch.

*The working chart for the design. Each square represents two threads of the canvas*

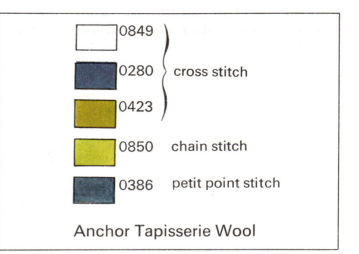

| | | |
|---|---|---|
| 0849 | } | |
| 0280 | } | cross stitch |
| 0423 | } | |
| 0850 | | chain stitch |
| 0386 | | petit point stitch |

Anchor Tapisserie Wool

33

# A beauty of a bag

Make no mistake about it, this is not just another shoulder bag! A roomy canvas work 'pouch' in rich colours combines a selection of not too difficult stitches with areas of padded leather, beads, tassels and macramé trim. The bag can be made on a more or less ambitious scale: work just one side of the canvas and the other in a complementary shade of hessian, or repeat the design on canvas for the second side. Either way, the result is a handsome—and useful—accessory.

## For the bag
**approx 41·3cm (14½in) by 32·5cm (12¾in) both sides worked on canvas**

### You will need
- □ 0·70m (¾yd) single thread canvas, at least 46cm (18in) wide (10 holes to 2·5cm (1in)
- □ Plain colour fabric for lining
- □ 2 tapestry needles, large and medium
- □ Black thin-line marking pen
- □ Indelible thin-line marking pen in neutral colour (ie medium grey)
- □ 1 large sheet of tracing paper
- □ Scraps of red leather
- □ Scraps of felt for padding leather
- □ Terylene or nylon thread to match leather
- □ Wooden beads: large red, medium purple

### Colours and quantities of threads required for the bag
- □ 25g (1oz) double knitting wool in each of the following colours: blue/mauve, deep blue, pink, warm pink, red, purple, dark blue/purple, dark red/purple, deep plum, tan
- □ 50g (2oz) double-double knitting wool (or substitute 4 strands of double knitting wool) in each of the following colours: pink/mauve, blue/pink, deep pink, deep plum, red, tan, yellow, orange
- □ 1 ball Anchor Mercer-Crochet, flesh 625
- □ 1 skein Anchor Soft Embroidery Cotton, buttercup 0297
- □ 5 skeins Anchor Stranded Cotton, 020 cardinal

## Method of working
Work each side of the bag—or only one, if the other side is to be of hessian or another sturdy fabric—on a frame. If possible, work the entire side at once; alternatively, half of the canvas may be rolled up and tied to one side of the frame.

## Transferring the design
Using the black marking pen, make a tracing of the entire design, repeating the panel with diamond shapes on the other side of the panel to include padded leather shapes. If just one side of the bag is to be worked on canvas, use only 0·45m (½yd) of canvas and 0·45m (½yd) of hessian; otherwise, repeat the design as a mirror image from the fold line.

Place the canvas over this tracing, mark out the design from the centre hole with the neutral-coloured marking pen and count the threads in each panel. Note that the side panels have a centre thread, and not a centre hole. The diamonds in the side panels are on a true cross of the canvas, although they appear somewhat distorted because the holes are not square. Another point to consider is the differing angles of the diagonals in the piece; these are indicated on the working chart. Allow at least 2.5cm (1in) turnings on all sides of the area to be worked.

The stitches to be used in each area are indicated on the working chart and stitch details are to act as a refresher for those unfamiliar or forgotten stitches.

## Padded areas
The leather shapes are applied after all stitching on the canvas has been completed. Draw the shape to be padded onto felt scraps, then cut out the shape fractionally smaller all round. For more raised padding, consecutively smaller layers of felt are cut out. The smallest piece of padding is stitched to the canvas first and then each larger layer in turn, the stitches going right through to

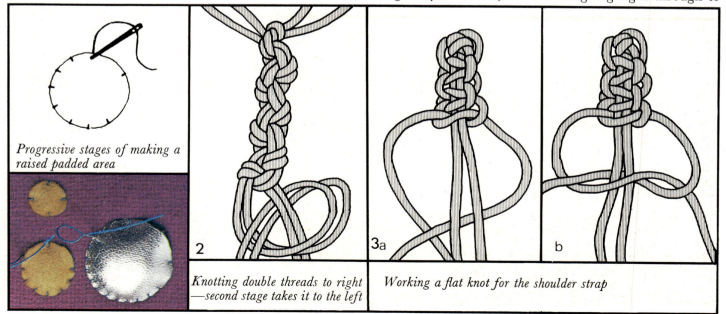

*Progressive stages of making a raised padded area*

2 *Knotting double threads to right —second stage takes it to the left*

3a b *Working a flat knot for the shoulder strap*

34

the background canvas (Figure 1). The leather shape is then pinned over the padding and secured with three or 4 stitches around the edge or in the corners. Complete the stitching all round, using stab stitch and working the stitches at right angles to the cut edge. Stitches should extend from this edge into shape.

**Finishing Touches**

The border along the top of the bag is a double knotted chain in macrame worked with pink double knitting wool (Figure 2). The shoulder strap is a flat knot braid in macrame worked in double-double knitting wool in red and deep plum (Figure 3). This braid should be long enough to extend down both sides of the bag.

The large wool pompons and tassels are simply made from double-double knitting wool, and with wooden beads, strung along the lower edge of the bag. If both sides are in canvas work, this edge will be a fold; if one side is fabric the lower edge will be a seam.

To line the bag, place the right sides of the lining fabric together and mark outline of the bag on one side. Machine or hand stitch just inside this line on 3 sides, leaving the top edge unstitched. Turn top edge over, slip the lining into the bag and slip stitch along the top edge.

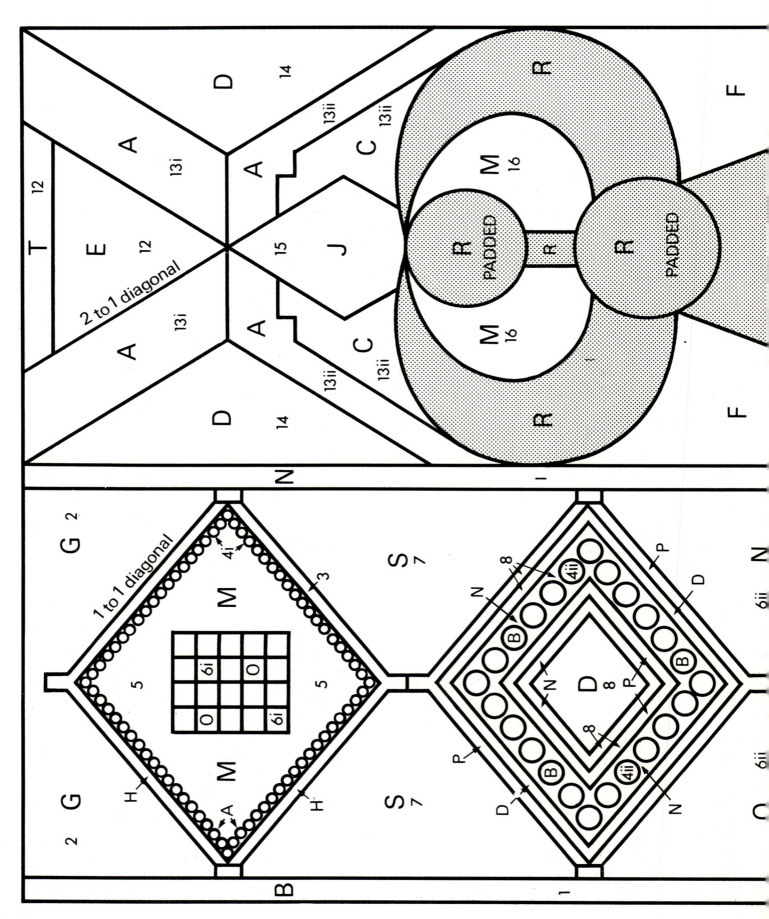

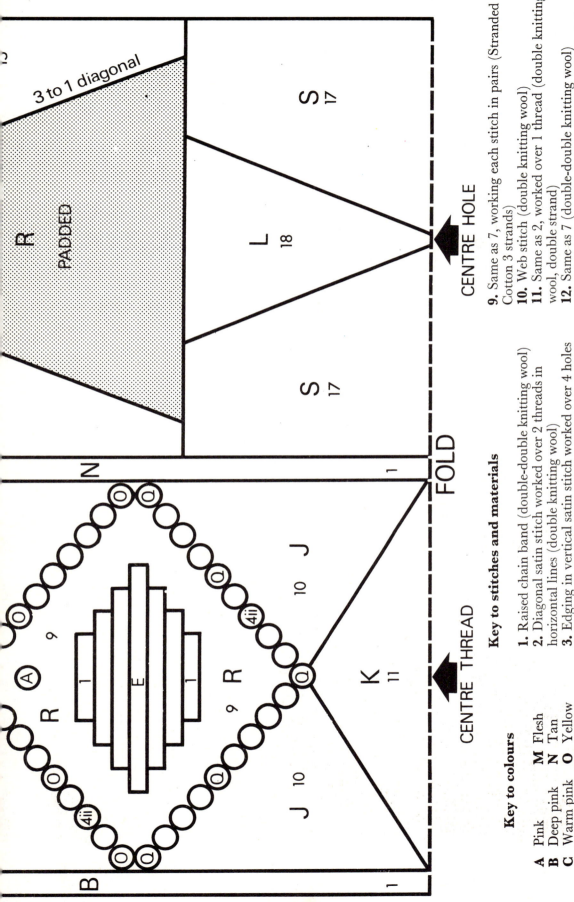

**3 to 1 diagonal**

PADDED

R

S 17

L 18

S 17

N

**FOLD**

CENTRE HOLE

CENTRE THREAD

J 10

R 9

K 11

J 10

B

**Key to colours**

| | | | |
|---|---|---|---|
| A | Pink | M | Flesh |
| B | Deep pink | N | Tan |
| C | Warm pink | O | Yellow |
| D | Orange | P | Gold |
| E | Pink/mauve | Q | Deep plum |
| F | Deep blue | R | Dark red |
| G | Blue/mauve | S | Red |
| H | Blue/pink | T | Violet |
| J | Purple | | |
| K | Dark blue/purple | | |
| L | Dark red/purple | | |

**Key to stitches and materials**

**1.** Raised chain band (double-double knitting wool)
**2.** Diagonal satin stitch worked over 2 threads in horizontal lines (double knitting wool)
**3.** Edging in vertical satin stitch worked over 4 holes (double-double knitting wool)
**4i.** French knots (double knitting wool)
**4ii.** Large French knots (double-double knitting wool)
**5.** Tent stitch (Mercer-Crochet)
**6i.** Diagonal satin squares worked over 3 holes (Soft Embroidery Cotton)
**6ii.** Same as 6i (double knitting wool)
**7.** Parisian stitch worked over 1 and 3 threads (double-double knitting wool)
**8.** Same as 3 (double knitting wool, double strand)
**9.** Same as 7, working each stitch in pairs (Stranded Cotton 3 strands)
**10.** Web stitch (double knitting wool)
**11.** Same as 2, worked over 1 thread (double knitting wool, double strand)
**12.** Same as 7 (double-double knitting wool)
**13i.** Cross stitch worked over 1 hole (double knitting wool)
**13ii.** Cross stitch worked over 3 holes (double knitting wool)
**14.** As 3, horizontal lines (double-double knitting wool)
**15.** Gobelin stitch worked over 5 holes (double knitting wool, double strand)
**16.** Same as 6 (Mercer-Crochet)
**17.** Same as 2 (double knitting wool)
**18.** Same as 3, worked in horizontal lines over 4 holes (double knitting wool, double strand)

# All aboard the petit-point express

Get up steam to make this delightfully original belt with its red locomotive and three carriages just about to pull into the little old-fashioned station. The belt is worked in petit point stitch and can be adjusted to fit most waist sizes.

## For the belt
**To fit a 66cm to 71cm (26in to 28in) waist:**

### You will need
☐ Anchor Tapisserie Wool in the following colours and quantities: 1 skein each of 0335 red, 0398 grey, 0399 dark grey, 0298 yellow, 0245 dark green, 0268 leaf green, 0403 black, 0123 mauve, 0871 maroon, 0148 navy blue, 0146 bright blue, 0352 mid-brown, 0358 peat brown, 0380 dark brown, 0427 tan; approx 2 skeins of 0508 sky blue; approx 3 skeins of 0243 grass green
☐ 0·90m (1yd) single thread canvas 16 holes to 2·5cm (1in), 58·5cm (23in) wide
☐ 0·90m (1yd) velvet for the lining
☐ 4 large press studs

### Method of working
The design is worked throughout in petit point stitch. Each row is worked so that it slopes in the opposite direction from the last, which prevents the canvas from warping.
The chart is divided into three sections—the engine, the tender and one carriage, and the station. Beginning at the left-hand end of the canvas, work about 5cm (2in) of plain grass and sky as shown at the front of the engine. Then work the engine following the chart and colour key. Work the tender and the mauve carriage next, joining them to the engine at the black link. Then work

*The engine, the tender and the three carriages can be seen when the belt is laid out flat*

the maroon and navy blue carriages in the same way. Add an area of plain grass and sky at the end as at the front of the engine. These plain sections can be lengthened as required to fit your waist measurement. Each square on the chart represents 4 stitches (2 horizontally by 2 vertically).
The station building is worked on a separate piece of canvas, as it forms the buckle of the belt.

### To make up
When the embroidery is complete, trim the canvas to within 1·5cm (⅝in) of the edge, and line both the belt and the station with the velvet. Sew a press stud to each corner of the velvet at the back of the station, and 2 to each end of the belt, adjusting the position as required.

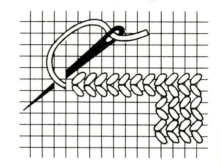

*Petit point stitch in alternately sloping rows*

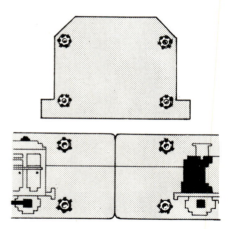

*Sew a press stud to each corner at the back of the station and two to each end of the belt*

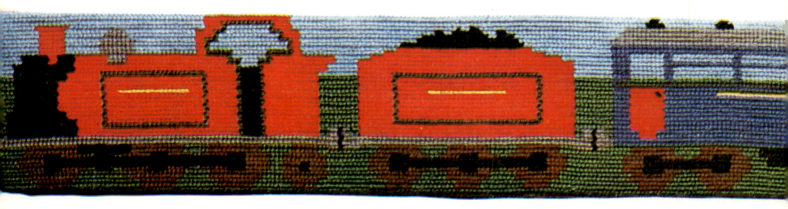

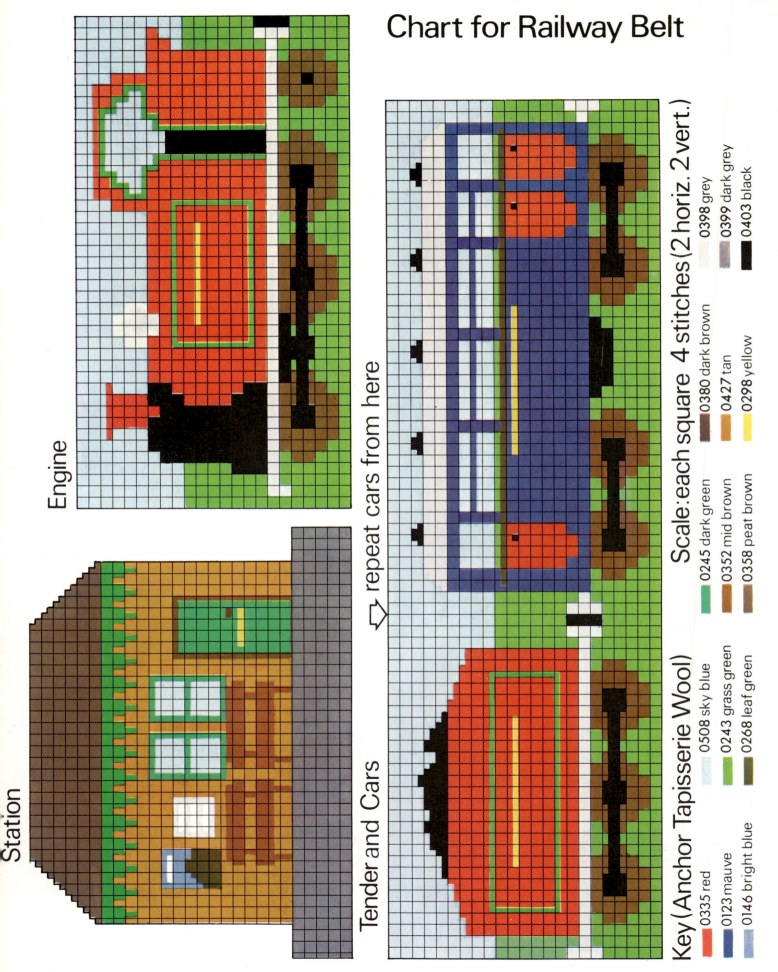

# Chart for Railway Belt

Engine

Station

Tender and Cars

→ repeat cars from here ⇨

**Scale: each square 4 stitches (2 horiz. 2 vert.)**

**Key (Anchor Tapisserie Wool)**

0335 red
0123 mauve
0146 bright blue
0508 sky blue
0243 grass green
0268 leaf green
0245 dark green
0352 mid brown
0358 peat brown
0380 dark brown
0427 tan
0298 yellow
0398 grey
0399 dark grey
0403 black

# Reflections on a frame

An unusual decorative idea for working a canvaswork border, is to frame a mirror with this highly original design in geometric patterns. Only three simple stitches are used to work the frame. The eye-catching effect is achieved by clever positioning of the stitches and interesting use of colour. Make the frame for either a stand-up mirror for your dressing-table, or for a hanging mirror.

## For the frame
**16·5cm by 21·5cm (6½in by 8½in)**

### You will need
- ☐ 0·3m (⅓yd) single thread canvas, 16 threads to 2·5cm (1in)
- ☐ Anchor Tapisserie Wool in the following colours and quantities: 2 skeins 0403 black, 1 skein each of 0402 white, 0497 grey, 0432 blue, 0982 light brown, 0340 rust
- ☐ Piece of mirror glass measuring 16·5cm by 21·5cm (6½in by 8½in)
- ☐ Copydex adhesive
- ☐ Piece of stiff cardboard 16·5cm by 21·5cm (6½in by 8½in)
- ☐ Strong thread for lacing the canvas
- ☐ Piece of felt 16·5cm by 21·5cm (6½in by 8½in) for the backing

### Method of working
The working chart indicates the stitches used and the direction in which they are worked. There are three different stitches used: tent stitch, petit point, and flat or cushion stitch. They are varied in direction to add interest to the design.

Use the illustration as a guide to placing the colours. The outer edge and the corners are worked in diagonal stripes of black and grey petit point. The zigzag border is worked in light brown, blue and rust. All the cushion stitch squares which form the inner border are worked in black or white, while the remaining squares of petit point are worked in black and white stripes. The tweed effect on the inside edge is achieved by working alternate black and white stitches.

**NB** Each corner and each long side of the frame is slightly different. The chart shows all four corners and part of the design on each side. To make the frame to the dimensions given, the design on each long side is repeated 6 times, and on each short side 4 times.

### To trim the canvas
Trim the canvas around the frame leaving 2cm (¾in) turnings. Cut out the centre of the canvas, again leaving 2cm (¾in) turnings. Make a diagonal cut at each inner corner, taking great care not to cut into the stitching. Fold back the inner turnings and stitch down.

### To make up the mirror frame
Cut out a piece of cardboard the same size as the mirror glass and make slits in it as shown. Fold the flap back along the dotted line so that it juts out to form a stand for the mirror. Glue the cardboard to the back of the mirror.

Glue the frame to the front edge of the mirror, lining up the edges of the work with the edges of the glass. Turn the outer turnings to the back and, using strong thread, lace across the back of the mirror horizontally and vertically. On the horizontal lacing, make holes in the cardboard flap with the needle and pass the thread through so that the lacing lies flat.

Cut out a piece of felt the same size as the mirror for the backing. Make a vertical slit down the middle for the stand to emerge and then oversew the felt to the frame, making sure that no unworked canvas is left showing.

Alternatively, to make a hanging mirror, omit the cardboard, and lace the canvas across the back of the mirror glass as before. Sew on a felt backing and attach two curtain rings to the top corners.

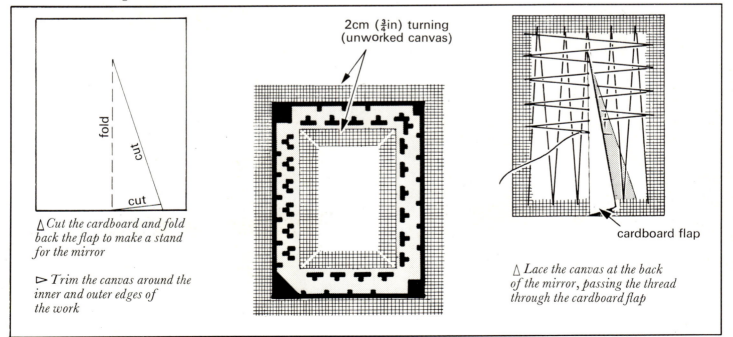

2cm (¾in) turning (unworked canvas)

cardboard flap

△ Cut the cardboard and fold back the flap to make a stand for the mirror

▷ Trim the canvas around the inner and outer edges of the work

△ Lace the canvas at the back of the mirror, passing the thread through the cardboard flap

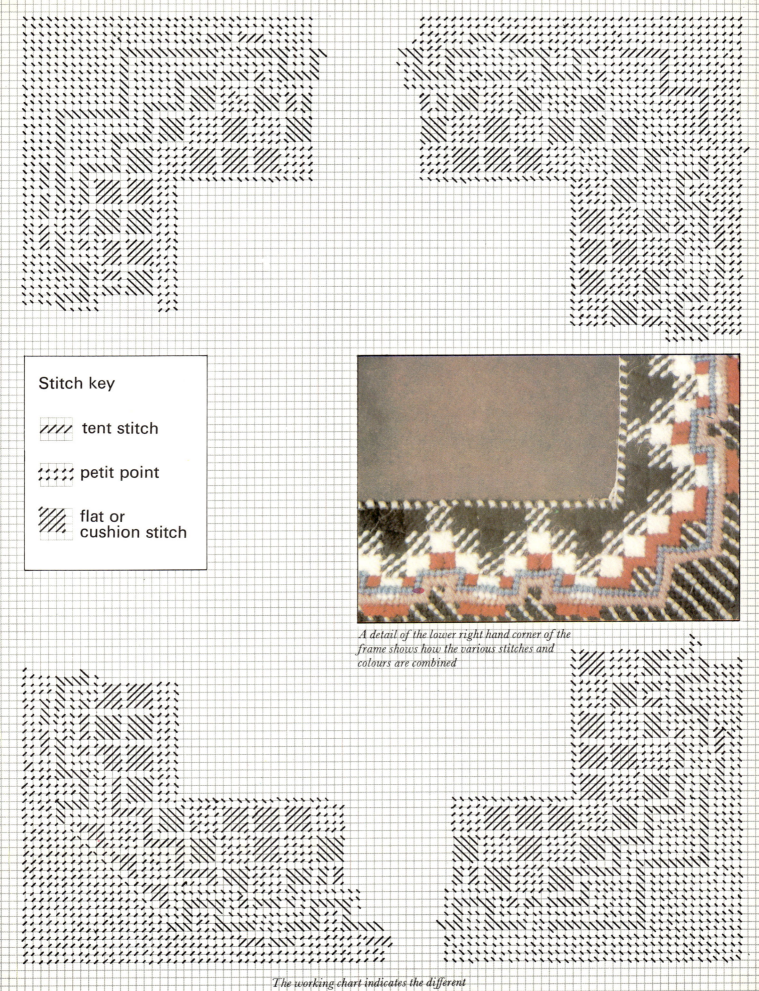

**Stitch key**

///// tent stitch

;;;;; petit point

///// flat or
cushion stitch

*A detail of the lower right hand corner of the frame shows how the various stitches and colours are combined*

*The working chart indicates the different stitches used*

# In the pink

Make this beautiful belt to brighten up the simplest of garments. Team it up to the greatest effect with a tunic top, an evening caftan or a catsuit. Any colour combination is suitable: shades of the same colour or brilliantly contrasting ones, perhaps chosen to wear with a specific garment.

## For the belt
0·25m (¼yd) 69cm (27in) or 0·90m (1yd) 60cm (23in) (depending on the waist size) single thread canvas (16 threads to 2·5cm (1in))

## You will need
☐ No 18 tapestry needle
☐ Anchor Soft Embroidery in the following colours and quantities
☐ 13 skeins·075 light old rose
☐ 7 skeins 078 dark old rose

## Method of working
The design can be extended in length to fit any waist measurement.

To give the most attractive results the entire design should be worked, although a simpler alternative is just to work the central motif, then fill in the remaining area in a single colour.

The design is worked in satin stitch, using Anchor Soft Embroidery. The trace pattern indicates the position of each colour in the design.

## Transferring the design
Place the traced pattern under the canvas and trace the design and the outline of the belt onto the canvas with an indelible marking pen or acrylic paints in a neutral colour. If desired, fill in the design with acrylic paints, using somewhat more subdued colours than those for the yarns to be used for working the design.

The design is repeated as a mirror image where indicated. Repeat as much of the secondary motif along the narrow portion of the belt as is required: a repeat of 1-1½ times on each side should be adequate. Allow at least 2·5cm (1in) at each end for turnings when making up.

Trace pattern for belt embroidery

Repeat this motif as required to accommodate waist measurement

# It's a frame up

All the colours of the rainbow are worked into this eye-catching canvaswork picture frame. Using only 3 simple stitches, the frame would make an ideal project for a beginner, although the most experienced needle-woman would enjoy working such a variety of colours. We chose an arrangement of pressed spring flowers to echo the frame's bright colours, but it would look equally good surrounding a mirror or any favourite picture.

## For the frame
**30·5cm (12in) square**

### You will need
- ☐ 0·5m (½yd) single thread canvas, 16 threads to 2·5cm (1in)
- ☐ Anchor Tapisserie Wool in the following colours and quantities: 4 skeins 0162 blue, 3 skeins 013 red, 2 skeins each 0239 green, 0295 yellow, 0314 orange, 0106 purple; 1 skein 096 mauve
- ☐ Piece of glass measuring 30·5cm (12in) square
- ☐ Copydex adhesive
- ☐ Piece of stiff cardboard 30·5cm (12in) square
- ☐ Piece of felt 30·5cm (12in) square for backing
- ☐ Strong thread for lacing the canvas
- ☐ Two small curtain rings

## Method of working
The working chart shows the stitches used and the direction in which they are placed. Only three stitches are used: tent stitch, petit point and flat or cushion stitch. The variety of colours and the direction in which the stitches are worked add interest and texture.

Use the photograph as a guide to placing the colours. Diagonal stripes of petit point around the inner and outer edges add a pretty beading effect to the frame. When working the corners, make sure to follow the chart carefully as all the petit point squares are worked in different directions.

**NB** The centre stitches of the top and bottom are arranged slightly differently from those at the sides, as is shown on the chart.

## To trim the canvas
Trim the canvas around the frame leaving 2cm (¾in) turnings. Cut out the centre of the canvas, again leaving 2cm (¾in) turnings. Make a diagonal cut at each inner corner, taking great care not to cut into the stitching. Fold back the inner turnings and stitch down.

## To make up the picture frame
Cut out a piece of cardboard the same size as the frame. Place your picture over the cardboard and the piece of glass over the picture. Glue the frame to the edge of the glass, lining up the outer edges of the work with the edges of the glass. Turn the outer turnings to the back and, with strong thread, lace across the back of the picture horizontally and vertically. Back the frame with felt.

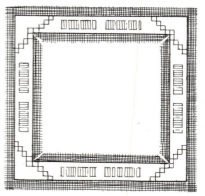

*Trim the canvas around the inner and outer edges of the work, leaving a 2cm (¾in) turning of unworked canvas*

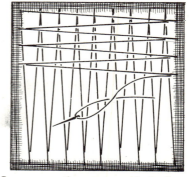

*Lace across the canvas at the back of the picture*

# Stitch chart for frame

*A detail of one corner of the frame shows how the colours and stitches are combined*

## Stitch key

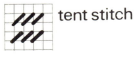 tent stitch

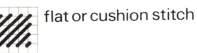 flat or cushion stitch

petit point

*The working chart indicates the different stitches used and the direction in which they are worked*

centre of side

47

# Canvaswork pockets

Abstract flower shapes worked on a chequerboard background make these smart pockets for a jersey coatdress. Jackets, waistcoats and jeans can all be brightened up by the addition of one or more of these pockets, worked in attractive subtle shades.

## For two pockets
**each measuring 11·4cm (4½in) by 12·7cm (5in)**

### You will need
☐ 0·25m (¼yd) single thread canvas, 16 threads to 2·5cm (1in)
☐ Anchor Tapisserie Wool in the following quantities and colours: 2 skeins each 0504 light grey, 0497 blue grey, 0498 rose beige; 1 skein each 0388 gold, 0392 beige, 0438 grey green, 0428 rust, 0982 grey, 0380 dark brown, 0399 pewter, 0871 plum

*Adapt the size of the design for various uses*

## Method of working

Follow the working chart given for one of the pockets; then work the other pocket as a mirror image of this design. As the design is asymmetrical, the two pockets are thus evenly balanced.

The key to the working chart indicates colours and stitches to be used in the design. Tent stitch, petit point and flat or cushion stitch are the only stitches required and the varying direction of some stitches adds interest to the design.

## Adjusting the design

In order to increase or decrease the dimensions of the pockets, substitute canvas with a smaller or larger grid. The size and shape of the design can also be adjusted by altering the number of stitches in the border. Make whatever colour changes or substitutions are required to co-ordinate the pockets with a particular garment.

## Alternative uses

To make a pincushion, decorative box top, mirror back or cover for an address book, work the design on single thread canvas with 18 threads to 2·5cm (1in).

Or work 4 or more panels and sew them together to make a stool cover, perhaps trimming it with braid or cord to match the stitched border. As before, alter the border area to achieve the size required.

*A detail of the pocket shows the worked canvas before making up*

# Key

| | |
|---|---|
| Background: | light grey 0504 |
| | blue grey 0497 |
| Border : | rose beige 0498 |
| | light grey 0504 |
| | gold 0388 |
| | beige 0392 |
| Flowers : | grey green 0438 |
| | gold 0388 |
| | rust 0428 |
| | grey 0982 |
| Flower centres : | dark brown 0380 |
| | pewter 0399 |
| | plum 0871 |
| | grey green 0438 |
| Stitches : | Tent stitch |
| | Petit point |
| | Flat or cushion stitch |

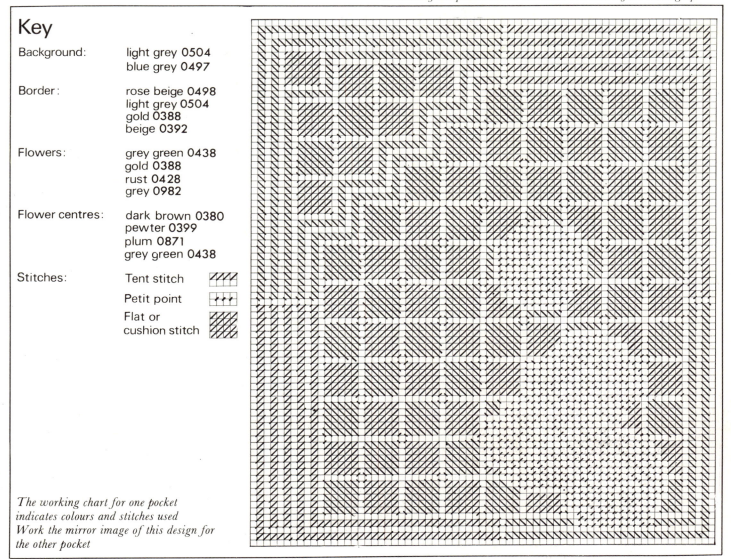

*The working chart for one pocket indicates colours and stitches used Work the mirror image of this design for the other pocket*

# A Danish rose

Cross stitch is one of the oldest forms of embroidery. For centuries it has been used in traditional European folk and peasant embroideries to decorate national costumes and household articles. Each country has developed its own particular style to such an extent that it is possible to determine where a particular piece of work or design originated. For instance, modern Danish cross stitch designs usually depict forms in a very realistic manner. The rounded shapes of the flowers, birds and animals are embroidered in delicate pretty colours in carefully selected tones which, when worked together, enhance this realistic effect. This delightful rose motif is typical of the Danish style in cross stitch, and can be used in many exciting ways. Here it is shown worked in two ways to create completely contrasting effects. One rose is worked in chunky yarns on canvas, the other in stranded embroidery cotton on fine linen and mounted in a tiny gold frame. To work a traditional design is sometimes a welcome change.

Worked in linen with 24 threads to 2·5cm (1in) over 2 threads each way the rose will measure about 6·4cm (2½in) by 6·4cm (2½in).

Worked as a cushion the same motif measures about 19cm (7½in) by 19cm (7½in)—the different scale is achieved by working the cross stitch over 3 threads each way on single weave canvas with 12 threads to 2·5cm (1in), using 2 strands of tapestry wool.

# Bolero to match all moods

Make this beautiful bolero to suit every occasion. Wear it with a flowing gipsy skirt and blouse for a romantic mood. Transform a classic camel polo neck jumper and trousers into a striking outfit, or add a touch of spice to a plain long-sleeved day dress in a toning colour. The bolero is straightforward to make and is worked in gros point stitch.

## For the Bolero
### To fit 86·5cm to 91·5cm (34 to 36in)

### You will need
- ☐ Anchor Tapisserie Wool in the following colours and quantities: 6 skeins 0429 pink; 5 skeins each of 0388 ecru, 0873 plum; 4 skeins each of 028 carnation, 0402 white; 3 skeins 0577 cyclamen
- ☐ 1·25m (1⅜yd) double thread canvas, 48·5cm (19in) wide, 10 holes to 2·5cm (1in)
- ☐ 1·1m (1¼yd) matching lining fabric 90cm (36in) wide
- ☐ 0·7m (¾yd) matching light woollen fabric 90cm (36in) wide for back of bolero
- ☐ 3·2m (3½yd) matching braid, 2·5cm (1in) wide
- ☐ Tapestry frame with 58·5cm (23in) tapes
- ☐ One Milward 'Gold Seal' tapestry needle No 18

### Working trammed gros point stitch
The design is worked throughout in trammed gros point stitch as shown in the diagrams. In diagram 1, work a trammed stitch from left to right, then pull the needle through and insert again up and over the crossed threads. In diagram 2, pull the needle through on the lower line two double threads (vertical) to the left in readiness for the next stitch.

As the canvas is tightly stretched on a frame, you will need to use both hands for working. With the right hand on top of the canvas, insert the needle downwards through the canvas, pulling it through with the left hand. With the left hand, push the needle upwards through the canvas, pulling it out with the right hand.

### Method of working
Cut two pieces from the canvas, each measuring 63cm by 48·5cm (24¾in by 19in) and mark the centre of each piece both horizontally and vertically with a line of basting stitches. Mount the first piece of canvas in the frame with the raw edges to the tapes.

The chart gives the complete left front of the bolero, indicating the areas of different colours. The central lines are indicated by arrows which should coincide with the basting stitches. Each background square on the chart represents the double thread of the canvas.

Commence the design centrally and work following the

*Trim round the canvas except for the dart, leaving 1·5cm (⅝in) turnings on the shoulder and side seams.*
*Pin the braid to the right side of the bolero, folding it under so that half shows on the right side and half on the wrong side*

chart, using the letter and sign key to place the colours. To work the right side, mount the second piece of canvas in the frame and repeat the design in reverse.

### Stretching the canvas and cutting out
The canvas may require stretching when removed from the frame. Dampen the canvas, then pin it to a clean dry board pulling it gently to the correct shape. Leave to dry naturally.

Trim round the canvas except for the dart, leaving 1·5cm (⅝in) turnings on the shoulder and side seams. Trim as close to all the other edges as possible, taking care not to cut into the stitching. Make the pattern for the back of the bolero, enlarging from the layout diagram onto squared paper, and cut out the woollen fabric and the lining. Cut the lining for the two front pieces using the worked canvas plus the unworked borders as a guide.

Stitch the darts on the bolero fronts, either by machine or using a firm back stitch. Slash up the centre of the darts and press open with a slightly damp cloth and a medium hot iron. Stitch the darts on the back of the bolero and join the canvas and the woollen material at the side and shoulder seams. Press seams open. Stitch the lining in the same way, then place the bolero and the lining together wrong sides facing. Tack round the edge of the bolero and round the armholes, matching seams. Machine stitch 0·6cm (¼in) in from all the edges.

Edge the bolero with braid as follows. Turn under 1·5cm (⅝in) at one end of the braid and start pinning it to the right side of the bolero from a side seam, folding it so that half shows on the right side and half on the wrong side. Pin all round the edges of the bolero and the armholes, then neaten the end by again turning it under 1·5cm (⅝in) and stitching it to join at the seam. Stitch the braid on the right side, and to the lining using a small hem stitch.

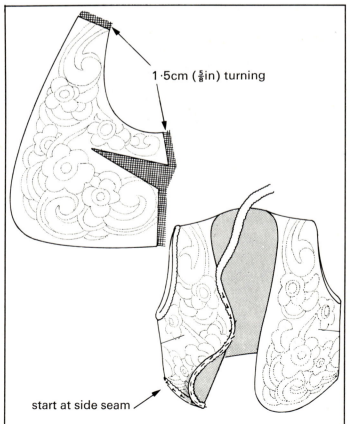

1·5cm (⅝in) turning

start at side seam

# Graph pattern for Back

Back

Fold

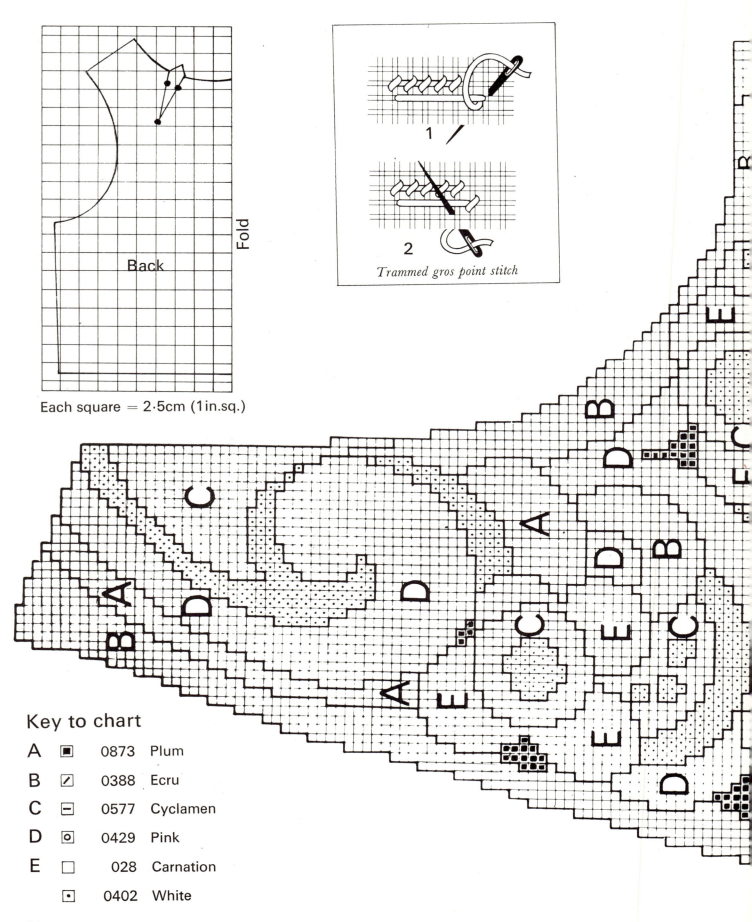

Trammed gros point stitch

Each square = 2·5cm (1in.sq.)

## Key to chart

| | | | |
|---|---|---|---|
| A | ▣ | 0873 | Plum |
| B | ⧄ | 0388 | Ecru |
| C | ⊟ | 0577 | Cyclamen |
| D | ⊙ | 0429 | Pink |
| E | ☐ | 028 | Carnation |
| | ⊡ | 0402 | White |

# Working chart for left front of Bolero
Reverse for right front

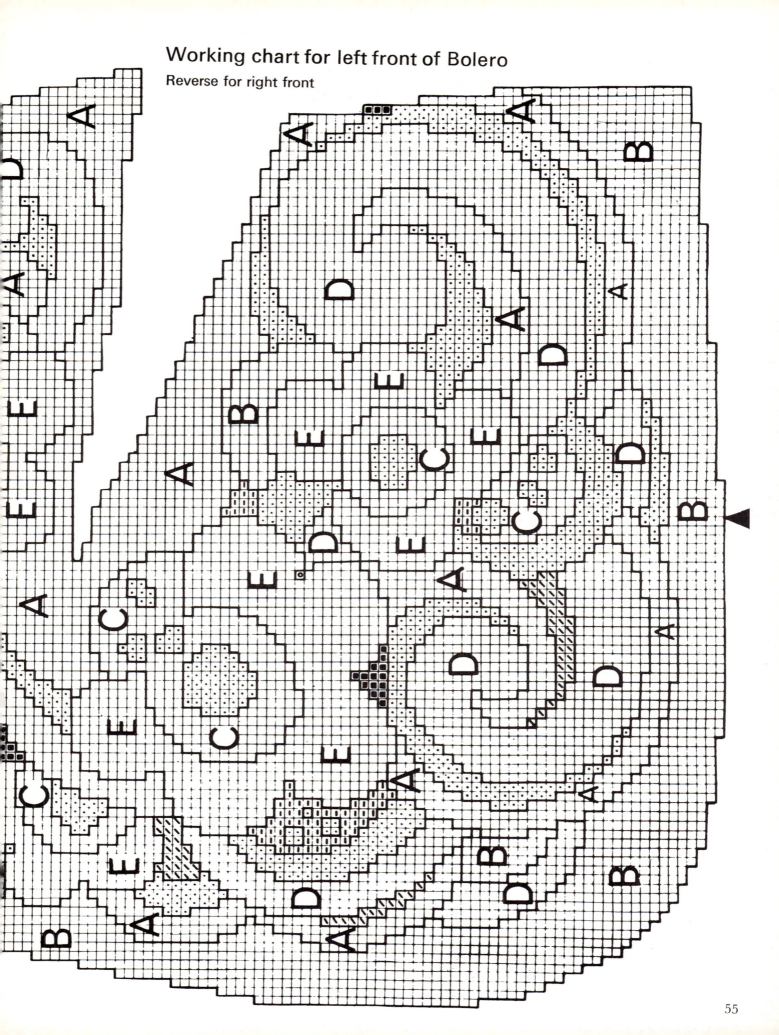

55

# Art Deco cushion

'Lamp stands' is a bold design for a canvas work cushion. Work the entire design in horizontal and vertical rows of satin stitch.

## For the cushion
### 41·3cm (16¾in) by 30cm (11¾in)

## You will need
☐ 0·45m (½yd) single thread canvas, 16 holes to 2·5cm (1in)

☐ DMC Tapestry Wool, Article 482 in the following quantities and colours:
6 skeins 7501 beige; 2 skeins 7435 yellow; 6 skeins 7146 salmon; 7 skeins 7317 blue

☐ Cushion pad or Terylene wadding

☐ Fabric in toning colour for backing

## Method of working
Following the working chart for the design, use the stitches and colours designated in the key. The chart gives one half the design to be worked; repeat as a mirror image where indicated.

## Alternative colours
In order to complement another colour scheme with the cushion, substitute these shades in D.M.C. Tapestry Wool: 7351 pale green, 7436 gold, 7363 olive green and 7307 dark blue.

*The working chart for the colour scheme illustrated is shown overleaf and the alternative colour scheme is shown below or you can choose a colour combination of your own*

## Key to working chart

| | |
|---|---|
| ☐ | **7501** beige vertical satin stitch |
| ☐ | **7146** salmon horizontal satin stitch |
| ☐ | **7317** blue vertical satin stitch |
| ☐ | **7435** yellow horizontal satin stitch (strips between bulbs – vertical satin stitch) |

## Key to alternative colour chart

| | |
|---|---|
| ☐ | **7363** olive green |
| ☐ | **7307** dark blue |
| ☐ | **7351** pale green |
| ☐ | **7436** gold |

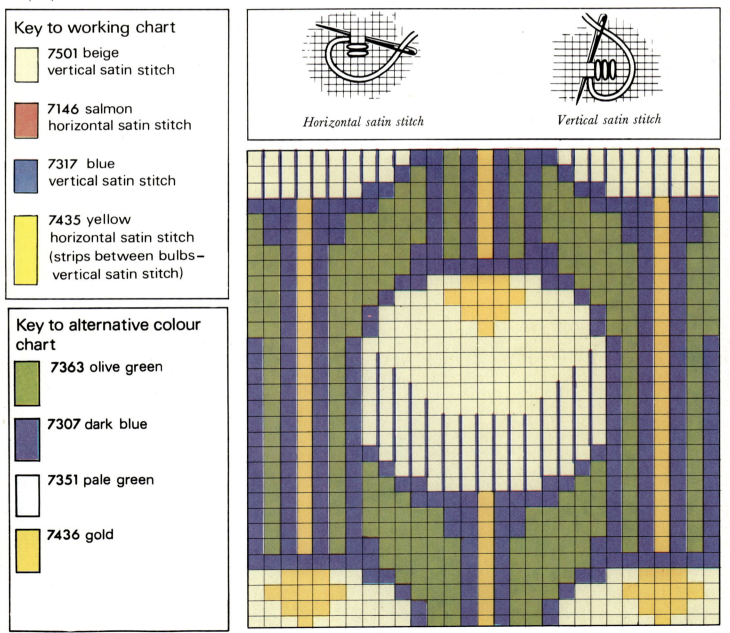

*Horizontal satin stitch*          *Vertical satin stitch*

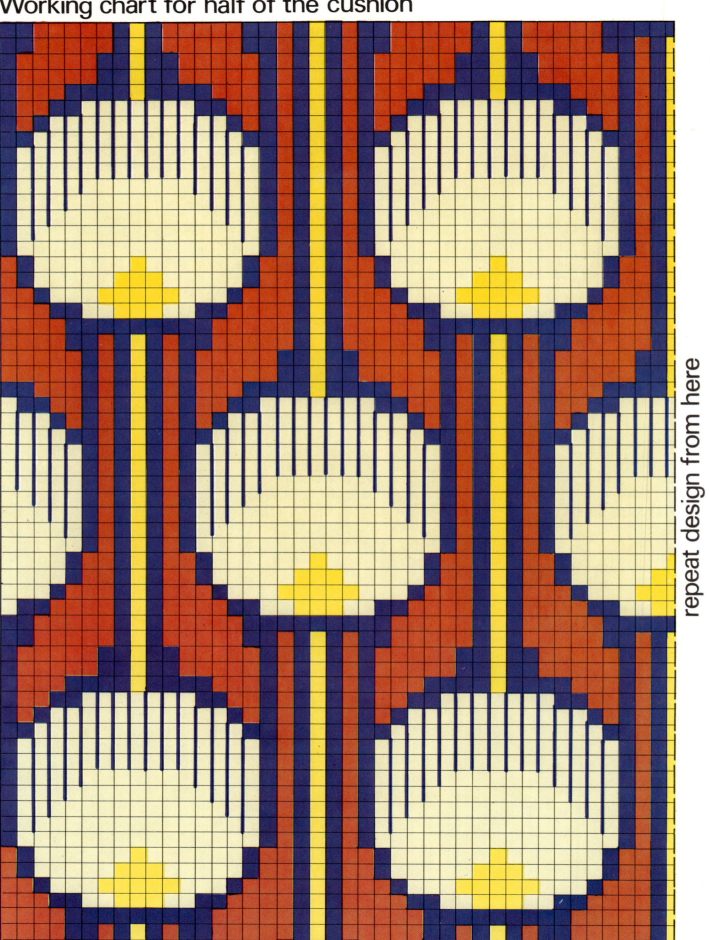

repeat design from here